Digital Discipleship & Evangelism

A practical guide for outreach, community service, growth, and evangelism for conferences, local churches, and personal ministries.

Jamie Domm

Digital Discipleship & Evangelism

Author: Jamie Domm
Editor: Georgia Damsteegt
Design and layout: Christal Gregerson

Available from:
Advent*Source*
5120 Prescott Avenue
Lincoln, NE 68506
402.486.8800
AdventSource.org

Printed in the United States of America

ISBN # 978-1-62909-777-0

Acknowledgements

"You will seek me and find me when you seek me with all your heart."
– Jeremiah 29:13, NIV

"I planted the seed, Apollos watered it, but God has been making it grow."
– 1 Corinthians 3:6, NIV

Everyone has a part to play in spreading the gospel and making it accessible to seekers, but ultimately, God's divine hand is what produces the fruit. We know that no accomplishment, large or small, is possible without the Holy Spirit. May He continue to guide our Church as we strive to accomplish our great commission in the modern age.

I am continuously impressed by the creativity and the passion of the digital missionaries in the Adventist community. Many of them have inspired passages in this guidebook and deserve special recognition for their valuable contributions to the digital mission field. They include, in no particular order, Rachel Lemons Aitken, Kaleb Eisele, Dee Casper, Justin Khoe, Amie Regester, Erica Jones, Ryan Becker, Matthew Lucio, Felecia Datus, Leslie Samuel, Amy Prindle, and Jason Alexis. There are many more who cannot be mentioned here. I pray that God blesses their efforts.

A huge thank you goes to Georgia Damsteegt for her astute editing skills, feedback, and perspective, which helped shape this guidebook into an accessible tool for churches and ministries throughout the North American Division and beyond.

I deeply appreciate Alvin Kibble and Paul Hopkins for their confidence in me and for suggesting that I pursue this passion project. These men are truly invested in mentoring younger generations and shaping the future of the Church.

Special thanks to my dear husband, whose unwavering faith continues to inspire and motivate me. Without his love and encouragement, this project would not have been possible.

The Social Media + Big Data Department is eternally grateful for the support and foresight of our North American Division leadership as we seek to prioritize the use of technology at all levels of the Seventh-day Adventist Church, revolutionizing ministry delivery through the use of innovative digital media.

To friends, family, and colleagues, thank you for your support and prayers.

Blessings,

Jamie Domm
Digital Strategist
Social Media + Big Data, North American Division

I dedicate this book to my daughter, "Nugget,"
who has been my constant companion, muse,
and occasional saboteur throughout this project,
beginning in the womb. May she grow up steadfast
in the Lord and find her Church vibrant, relevant,
and prepared to meet her generation's needs.

Table of Contents

Engagers

Digital Disciples and Missionaries

Distributors

Part 3—What's Next?

About the Author

Jamie Domm has over 14 years' experience in developing and implementing results-focused digital marketing strategies for nonprofits. Most recently, she worked at the North American Division of Seventh-day Adventists for four years as the digital strategist for a new department, Social Media + Big Data, that connects members and mission through technology. During her time at the North American Division, she developed social media policies, devised comprehensive digital strategies for major initiatives, trained departments and ministries to run their own digital communications, helped launch new digital ministries, promoted conferences and events to increase attendance, and created an extensive resource website (SDAdata.org) for individuals, churches, conferences, and organizations interested in digital evangelism.

Previously, Mrs. Domm worked at Smithsonian Associates, the world's largest museum-based education program, where she contributed significantly to the Associates' becoming revenue neutral for the first time in 50 years. While with the Baltimore Symphony Orchestra earlier in her career, she received national recognition for her work in the emerging field of digital strategy, and the orchestra was recognized for its technological achievements in communications.

Mrs. Domm is dedicated to creating digital disciples and believes that the next Great Awakening will be online. She conducts online trainings, speaks at conferences, and advocates for young digital missionaries. Committed to training and mentoring young people, she offers guidance and coaching to those interested in digital communications or evangelism.

Mrs. Domm is also an accomplished musician, student of the Bible, and avid reader. She was baptized into the Seventh-day Adventist church in 2007 and lives with her husband and daughter in Virginia. She frequently appears as a panelist on "Hope Sabbath School."

Introduction

This guidebook reframes what you may already know regarding discipleship and evangelism with updates to reflect the realities of a digital-centric social structure. These concepts are nothing new, and in fact, these ideas are built on the shoulders of history's evangelistic giants for application in the modern world. This book serves as a practical guide for applying Biblical concepts of effective discipleship and evangelism in the digital space. We must rethink how we share the gospel message to effectively utilize the innovative tools and technologies freely available to all of us. The platforms and tools will change, but the principles will not, because they are all grounded in Biblical examples.

Local churches are uniquely positioned to combine traditional methods with technology to amplify the gospel message throughout the greater community. Merging the two allows us to be more effective at serving people locally and creating meaningful connections. Digital communication strategies are highly customizable to your organization's needs and mission. How these strategies play out in your congregation will depend entirely on the members of your congregation, your resources (human, financial, and available technologies), and what makes the most sense for your community.

Individually, we are all called to discipleship, and in the modern world, that means putting Jesus on display in our sphere of influence, both digital and analog. It doesn't matter if you have 4 or 40,000 friends or followers online; you have influence. How we use our social influence matters. This series will also outline how individuals can use their creativity alongside technical skills as well as the digital tools you hold in your hand for kingdom building.

This guide seeks to act as a catalyst for a cultural shift towards prioritizing technology in the Seventh-day Adventist Church at all levels. We can revolutionize ministry delivery through use of innovative technology. To accomplish this, we must start with recognizing the need for and legitimacy of digital mission work. The Social Media + Big Data department is pleased to share with you a model and provide recommendations on how the Church can embrace digital evangelism and discipleship at an individual, church, and corporate level.

Part 1
The Digital World

The Model

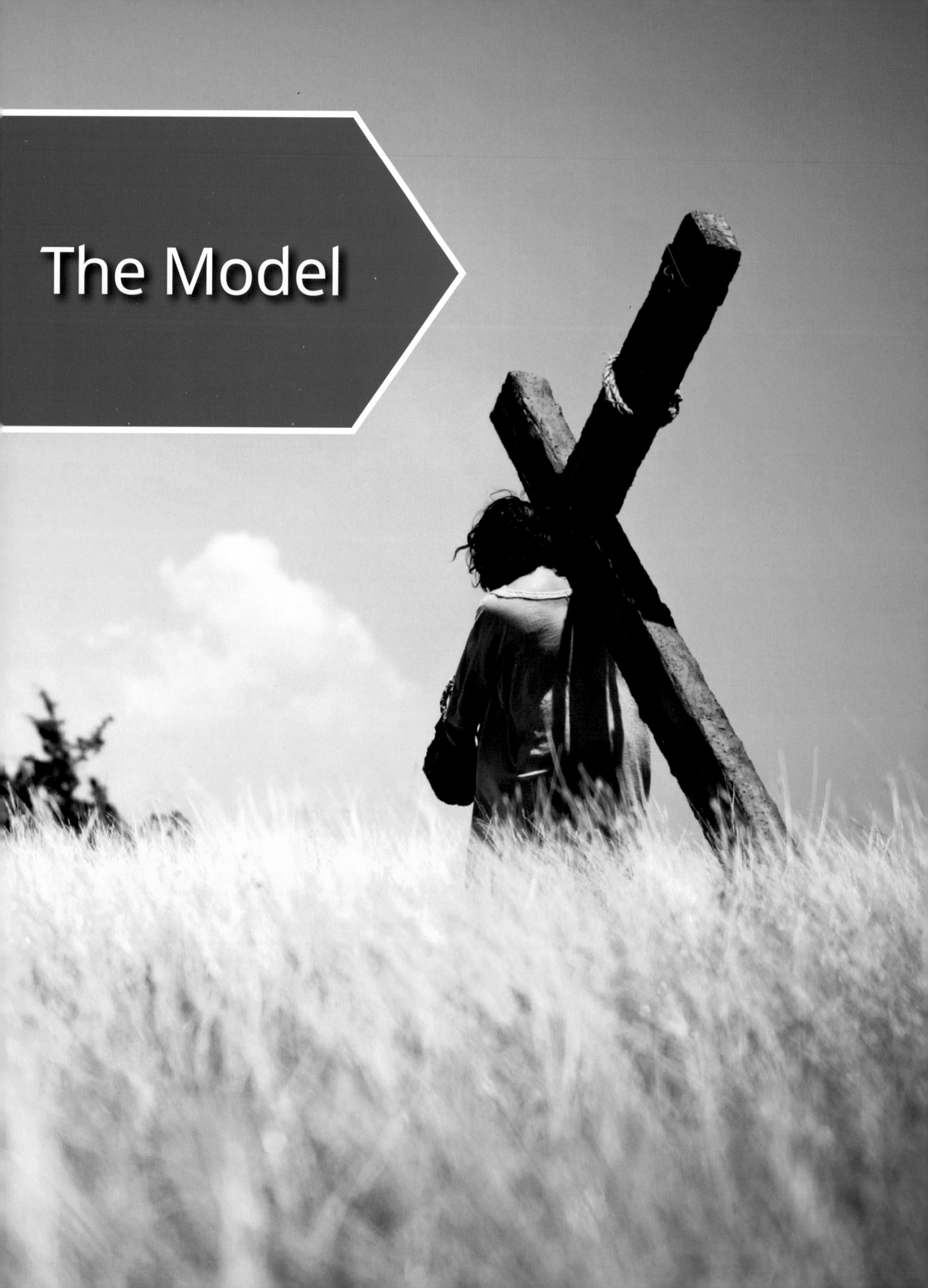

What Does It Mean to Be a Digital Missionary?

With the explosion of creative and tech savvy Christians trying their hand at digital mission work, many new terms have been added to the Christian vocabulary to describe this type of ministry. To make sure we understand the differences and similarities between them, it is worth taking time to create clear definitions. As children of God we are all called to do His work, and many find it useful to define their practical role in sharing the gospel—helping to shape their goals, find purpose, and communicate their mission to others.

"Therefore go and make disciples of all nations, baptizing them in the name of the Father and of the Son and of the Holy Spirit, and teaching them to obey everything I have commanded you. And surely I am with you always, to the very end of the age" (Matthew 28:19-20).

evangelism

noun

evan·ge·lism | \ i-ˈvan-jə-ˌli-zəm \

Evangelism is generally understood as the act of publicly preaching the gospel and the teachings of Jesus Christ to persuade people to adopt a Christian worldview. The word evangelist comes from the Koine Greek word εὐαγγέλιον (transliterated as euangelion) and originally meant a reward given to the messenger for good news but later came to just mean "good news" (Wikipedia).

Evangelism, then, by extension, can be understood as publicly sharing the good news. The way it is packaged and delivered may change, but as long as the gospel is being shared, it is evangelism.

Digital marketing is the promotion of products, services, causes, or ideas in the online space using digital technologies and tools such as the internet, social media, paid display ads, website platforms, and mobile phones.

Therefore, **digital evangelism** is defined as promoting the good news of the gospel and the teachings of Jesus Christ in the digital space using corresponding technologies to persuade others to adopt Christian beliefs. A digital evangelist is one who engages in **digital evangelism** as defined above.

With this in mind, how should digital discipleship be defined?

disciple

noun

dis·ci·ple | \ di-ˈsī-pəl \

Definition of disciple according to Merriam-Webster:

one who accepts and assists in spreading the doctrines of another.

In this context, a digital disciple is one who accepts and assists in the spreading of the doctrines of Christ through the use of digital tools in the digital space. However, digital discipleship is not limited to digital spaces but can, and often should, intersect with the physical world through the services offered. If we follow Jesus' example as a model for discipleship, we should expand this definition to include showing genuine interest in people and seeking to fulfill their mental, physical, and spiritual needs before inviting them to follow Christ and adopt His principles.

To do that, we have modified the definition of digital discipleship, as first presented by Rachel Lemons Aitken, *Digital Discipleship in the Seventh-day Adventist Church*, to be:

> *Digital discipleship a way to build relationships, meet the needs of the community, and advance the gospel message in the digital space, around a digital need or by utilizing a digital tool.*

missionary

noun

mis·sion·ary | \ ˈmi-shə-ˌner-ē

Definition of missionary according to Merriam-Webster:

a person who undertakes a religious mission.

Religious missions are traditionally seen as a means to promote Christianity, or another religion, in a foreign country. However, a **digital missionary** is one who shares their faith and beliefs in the digital space with digital tools and technologies, without being physically confined to a single geographical location. Digital missions are evangelistic campaigns that leverage digital tools and spaces for the distinct purpose of attracting converts to the faith. Digital evangelists, disciples, and missionaries all engage in **digital mission** work.

Digital bible workers utilize digital technologies to share the gospel and stimulate religious thought by creating and packaging content that addresses relevant needs/ questions and encourages people to advance in their spiritual journey. Digital bible workers build relationships with those in the broader community, online and offline, and usually within a specific geo-location territory, in order to create opportunities for one-on-one or small group Bibles studies held in person or via digital tools. They work in partnership with a local church and pastor to evaluate the needs of a community and determine relevant opportunities for outreach and service. They mentor converts in their development of Christian character and commitment to faith as well as train and equip new members for active discipleship roles. This role encompasses a mix of digital discipleship and evangelism to bridge the gap between working in the digital mission field and achieving real-world impact.

Why Is Digital Discipleship and Evangelism Needed?

Digital discipleship and evangelism are ways to activate the social influence of a church membership, building bridges to the local community, developing a meaningful understanding of felt needs, and determining relevant ways to serve the community (both in and outside the church). It's also a strategy to scale up friendship evangelism and empower individuals to be actively involved in the larger goals and mission of your church.

It's a way to reach seekers, especially young seekers.

As of 2017, the average person spends around two hours a day on social media, which adds up to **5 years and 4 months spent over a lifetime**[1]. When social media was ranked against other daily activities, it revealed that the average person will spend almost **three times as much**[2] time socializing on social media as opposed to socializing in person. The **average adult spends most of their waking hours behind a screen**[3] for work, entertainment, education, and socializing.

These averages are across all age demographics. When we only look at people under 30, a dramatic increase in social and screen time spent is observed. Teens can occupy upwards of **9 hours a day on social media** or **behind a screen**[4]. However, millennials can spend up to **18 hours a day consuming media**[5] in the form of movies, podcasts, social media, video games, reading, etc. This is an astounding amount of time spent on digital devices. Research studies vary, but it's clear that increased use is only limited by the confines of a 24-hour day, and basic human needs such as sleep.

Only **20% of Americans regularly attend church**[6], and only **2 in 10 millennials consider regular church attendance important**[7]. If we consider time spent "in church," a member who attends twice a week for a worship service and one other event only engages for four to five hours a week. How we respond to this reality either represents a challenge

1 Asano, Evan. "How Much Time Do People Spend on Social Media? [Infographic]." *Social Media Today*, 4 Jan. 2017, www.socialmediatoday.com/marketing/how-much-time-do-people-spend-social-media-infographic.

2 Asano, Evan. "How Much Time Do People Spend on Social Media? [Infographic]." *Social Media Today*, 4 Jan. 2017, www.socialmediatoday.com/marketing/how-much-time-do-people-spend-social-media-infographic.

3 Fottrell, Quentin. "People Spend Most of Their Waking Hours Staring at Screens." *MarketWatch*, MarketWatch, 4 Aug. 2018, www.marketwatch.com/story/people-are-spending-most-of-their-waking-hours-staring-at-screens-2018-08-01.

4 Anderson, Jenny. "Even Teens Are Worried They Spend Too Much Time on Their Phones." *Quartz*, Quartz, 23 Aug. 2018, qz.com/1367506/pew-research-teens-worried-they-spend-too-much-time-on-phones/.

5 McCarthy, Niall, and Felix Richter. "Infographic: Millennials Rack Up 18 Hours of Media Use Per Day." *Statista Infographics*, 13 Mar. 2014, www.statista.com/chart/2002/time-millennials-spend-interacting-with-media/.

6 Outreach Magazine. "7 Startling Facts: An Up Close Look at Church Attendance in America." *ChurchLeaders*, 19 July 2019, churchleaders.com/pastors/pastor-articles/139575-7-startling-facts-an-up-close-look-at-church-attendance-in-america.html.

7 "Study Analysis: 6 Reasons Why Only 2 in 10 Millennials Believe Church Attendance Is Important." The Christian Post, www.christianpost.com/news/study-analysis-6-reasons-why-only-two-in-10-millennials-believe-church-attendance-is-important-116882/.

or an untapped opportunity. These statistics may seem bleak for our mission, but there's another way to look at the situation.

How can we reach the 80%? Simple. We go and meet them where they spend their time, not where we want them to be. We have nine or more hours a day to connect with them. Part of this effort must utilize digital technologies to better understand behavior and needs before creating programs or resources that satisfy our assumptions about our target audience.

People are googling for God.

Each year there are millions of Google searches for answers to questions like:

- Is God real?
- What happens when we die?
- How do I know I'm saved?
- Why is there so much suffering in the world?

There is a great need for the Adventist message of hope and wholeness. Many people are hurting, entertaining suicidal thoughts, or feel there is no hope for their situation. They turn to the internet for companionship, understanding, information, anonymity, and more. It's easier for them to pour their hearts out online than it is to come to a friend, neighbor, co-worker, or family member.

Thirty thousand people search the keywords "church online" every month, and they mostly find opportunities to watch people in a building. People searching for answers need more than a program to watch.

At any given time, 22-28% of people are in crisis in the United States and Canada, says Samuel Neves, Associate Director of Communications, General Conference of Seventh-day Adventists. This amounts to 80 million+ people who need support. Crisis can be defined as loss of a loved one, illness, divorce, loss of a job, depression, drug addition, food insecurity, etc. For those who search for answers and comfort online, who is there to answer their questions and help them spiritually?

In addition, Neves says, the two main content categories people search online alone are religion and pornography. Both search categories are related to the need for relationships and connection. How can we steer seekers in a healthy direction?

90% of surveyed people[8] have used social media to communicate with a brand, and millennials prefer to reach out to an organization via social media rather than traditional channels like phone or email. This brings me to my next point: not everyone is ready to come to church; some are not even ready to discuss their issues in person. Over four million people visit North American Division church/ministry websites each year, and

8 Sprout Social. "The Sprout Social Index, Edition VI: Shunning Your Customers on Social?" *Sprout Social*, 7 May 2019, sproutsocial.com/insights/data/q2-2016/.

countless more engage on social media. The Church can be a voice that answers back to those seeking help through these channels and help open a door for a seeker's spiritual experience.

The digital mission field is vast and not restricted by geographical locations. 42% of the world's population[9] is on social media, and **77% of Americans**[10] are on social media. Every inhabited continent is represented in the digital space. While Christianity is on the decline in the West, it has never been easier to reach people. I believe the next Great Awakening will be a digital one, and reaching the digital mission field is our generation's great commission.

"Therefore go and make disciples of all nations, baptizing them in the name of the Father and of the Son and of the Holy Spirit, and teaching them to obey everything I have commanded you. And surely I am with you always, to the very end of the age" (Matthew 28:19-20).

---

9 Phipps, Brett, et al. "Digital in 2018: World's Internet Users Pass the 4 Billion Mark." *We Are Social*, 30 Jan. 2018, wearesocial. com/blog/2018/01/global-digital-report-2018.
10 Clement, J. "U.S. Population with a Social Media Profile 2019." *Statista*, 9 Aug. 2019, www.statista.com/statistics/273476/percentage-of-us-population-with-a-social-network-profile/.

The Digital Discipleship and Evangelism Model

A model for everyday ministry to real people and how to use social influence for kingdom building as it was demonstrated through the life of Jesus Christ.

During His three-and-a-half-year ministry, He:

- shared stories
- shared Godly (and scripture-based) wisdom
- attended to people's needs, physically and spiritually
- answered people's questions regarding spiritual matters and everyday challenges
- gave them hope
- created community
- developed an engaged/active church body
- lead people to wholeness
- equipped people to be disciples and to replicate the model He developed.

This model, when used for digital discipleship and evangelism, is a way we can follow Jesus' example, while utilizing modern tools and technologies. This approach is integrated, weaving traditional (analog) methods together with digital tools to magnify the scale of our efforts for wider impact in the physical world. For now, we're going to break down the digital components of the model. Later in this guidebook, we'll explore how digital can work together with traditional methods in the modern world.

A BASIC STRUCTURE FOR DIGITAL MINISTRIES CAN BE OUTLINED AS FOLLOWS

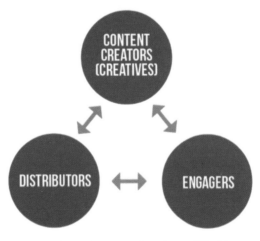

Credit: Digital Discipleship in the Seventh-day Adventist Church modified by Jamie Domm, Digital Strategist for the North American Division

In this model

- **Content creators** are those who package the gospel message and teachings of Jesus into various digital friendly formats such as: video, blogs, images, podcasts, etc.

- **Distributors** are organizations or individuals who use digital tools and technologies to share content within their sphere of digital influence.

- **Engagers** are empathic individuals within an organization, or operating independently, who engage in online conversations for the purpose of building meaningful relationships, better understanding needs, and determining meaningful ways to serve others in the community.

The two-way arrow in the chart indicates the overlap of skills and duties found within any ministry or church, as well as the necessity to curate digital content contributed by members (individuals or organizations) engaged in outreach and fellowship (distribution and engagement). Every organization should develop a strategic plan for digital outreach that covers these basic three elements. Individuals fall into at least one of the three categories but may serve in multiple capacities. Later in this guide we will unpack each of these categories in-depth and provide practical steps for implementation.

Individuals who are seeking to serve as digital missionaries can fulfill all these roles on their own or work within a network of digital missionaries to optimize reach, build community, and share content. By creating an ecosystem of digital missionaries, they can capitalize on each other's areas of specialty through mutual collaboration and shared social influence. A group of digital missionaries can learn as a group and adapt to changing technologies, increasing their ability to address relevant topics in a timely manner.

INDIVIDUAL DIGITAL MINISTRY

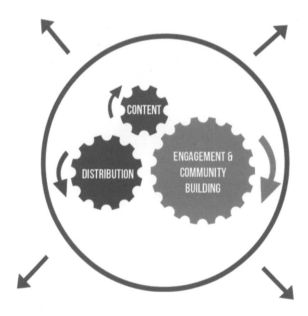

Credit: Graphic designed by Brittany McNitt

DIGITAL MINISTRY ECOSYSTEM

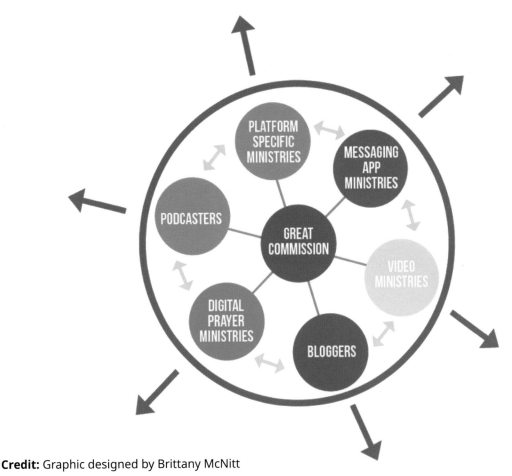

Credit: Graphic designed by Brittany McNitt

Organizations can provide structure for content creation that reflects the official mission and branding of a ministry. An organization should also develop a system for distribution internally and externally, as well as determine ways to tap into the reach potential of its members. Ministries can also set up teams of engagers who work within the brand structure to strengthen the relationships within the church community and/or who are trained to act independently as disciples, developing relationships outside of the Church for the purpose of evangelism. These organizations can also interact within the larger organizational structure of the Church to create a multilayered ecosystem of content creators, distributors, and engagers.

Each organizational level both creates and distributes content through their digital channels: up the chain, down the chain, and to the external audience. Each formal organization should also have a team of engagers to interact with the online community. In terms of the local conference and churches, the role of the engager will need to go beyond the digital space for in-person experiences.

The function of each layer of the Church can be summarized as follows

The Division serves in a creative role that specializes in developing sharable content, helping people solve problems, and addressing felt needs of those within the Adventist Church, as well as seekers. The goal is to share the gospel in relevant and culturally meaningful ways. The Division distributes this content down to the various levels of the Church's structure and to targeted individuals. A team of engagers actively responds to messages and builds community online to cultivate meaningful relationships with those it serves, bridging the gap between the individual and the perceived corporate brand.

Each **union and mission** creates and curates relevant content (from the Division, ministries, and other resources) for its territory, with a distribution mechanism to the Division and to its conferences with a people-care team (engagers) dedicated to building relationships with members and the community it serves.

Each **conference** is responsible for creating and curating content (from the Division, union, local churches, ministries, etc.) relevant to the needs of the churches, members, and communities it serves, distributing content and resources up to its union and out to its churches and communities. At the same time, it develops a care team (engagers) dedicated to building relationships with members and the community it serves. In the case of digital evangelism efforts, each role also endeavors to bring people to a real-world, in-person experiences through connections with relevant programs, bible studies, services, and more.

The **local church** can repurpose and create spiritual content to help move people through their spiritual journey, as well as address local and member needs, help solve problems, and seek to directly improve the well-being of the community. A church's distribution focus will be highly targeted to a geographical location and should leverage the social influence of its members. A committed team of engagers can build a 24/7 church experience for members and local community alike that answers questions and addresses felt needs in a timely and meaningful way.

Individual members of a church can serve in one or more roles as content creators (creatives), distributors, and engagers. As creatives, individuals can help package and develop church content in ways that are directly relevant to the community it serves. As distributors, the church body can function as a reach vehicle to their extended contacts by sharing and engaging with content. Empathic persons well suited to engagement can serve to strengthen the community within and outside the church. Individuals may also have their own personal ministry separate from their participation in the local church. Digital disciples can use their digital influence to share their thoughts, perspectives, testimonies, and faith experiences with their connections, while also proactively building relationships and improving the wellbeing of those they engage with through digital tools.

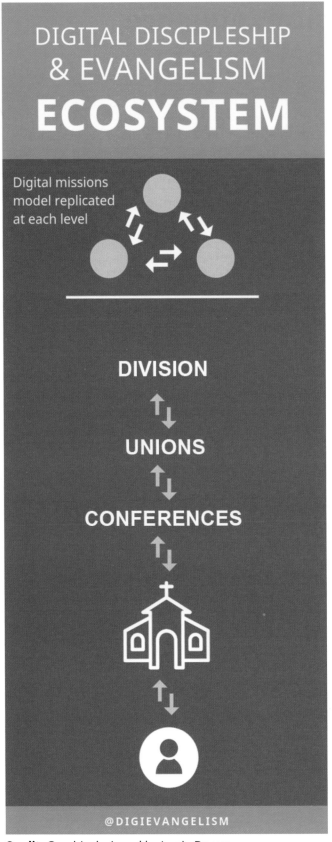

DIGITAL DISCIPLESHIP & EVANGELISM
ECOSYSTEM

Digital missions model replicated at each level

DIVISION

UNIONS

CONFERENCES

@DIGIEVANGELISM

Credit: Graphic designed by Jamie Domm

The Adventist Church should be on the cutting edge of preaching and teaching present truth. We have around 1.2 million members in the North American Division. What if every church (approximately 5,500) became a digital missions hub with those 1.2 million members also serving as creatives, distributors, and engagers? We, as the Church body, could work together as content creators, engagers, and distributors to generate a mighty voice for sharing the gospel message. There is a significant amount of untapped potential when you consider the social influence of every individual, church, ministry, school, conference, union, etc. We could overwhelm our corner of the digital space with truth, hope, and wholeness.

In order to catch up and realize this dream, we must prioritize technology at all levels of the Church's structure. We must become as effective as secular organizations in getting our message out and reaching our target audiences.

Turning Digital Influence into Global Impact

I am often asked if digital communications can really make a global impact when only around 42% (as of June 2019) of the world's population is on social media. This question always reminds me of one of my first campaigns for the Church.

In the summer of 2016, I worked with "Your Best Pathway to Health"[11] to help create community awareness for the free mega-health clinic that was coming to Beckley, WV, the heart of Appalachia. A quick search in Facebook Ads manager revealed that around 200K people within 50 miles of the convention center where the clinic would take place, were on Facebook. With a small budget of $200, I started a community awareness ad campaign targeted at those living within driving distance of Beckley. This digital effort was part of a larger multi-channel campaign that included newspaper ads, 30K+ hand-out flyers, and other traditional media.

Can We Really Reach Those People?

It is said that "familiarity breeds contempt" or, at least, presumptuous behavior. Soon after launching the campaign, I received a call from a long-time friend who felt very strongly that I was out of line to use Church funds for this digital campaign, and that I was out of touch with the realities of this community. After all, "this was Appalachia, and those people don't even have running water and electricity." After two hours of conversation, I still call her friend, because this was a teaching and learning moment. I had an opportunity to share the potential this technology offers for our mission, as well as gain a better understanding of the cultural paradigm I was up against (in terms of encouraging the Church to embrace digital strategies and the perceptions that may result). What she didn't know was that I made a decision based on data and not assumptions about the "least of these." In fact, she didn't know that I had been raised in the same economic class she felt I was so disconnected from.

I asked her one simple question: do you know someone who is not on social media? She said yes. I followed up with something like, "If you saw an online advertisement about free medical treatment with no strings attached, and you knew they needed help, would you tell them?" Without hesitation, she responded, "Of course!" One question and response summarized my strategy.

What I had done was make a strategic decision to activate the sharing power of the 200K people who were online and, most likely, connected to others in the community who were not on social media. It's human nature to share a good thing when we see it, especially with those we care about who need the services offered.

---

11 "Pathway to Health Coming to Indianapolis, Indiana!" Pathway To Health Volunteer Site, pathwaytohealthvolunteer.org/.

According to an extensive study conducted by the New York Times, **94% of people share content online because "they feel the content will improve the lives" of others.**[12] This act of sharing goes beyond the digital space.

> *"Then, leaving her water jar, the woman went back to the town and said to the people, 'Come, see a man who told me everything I ever did. Could this be the Messiah?' They came out of the town and made their way toward him" (John 4:28-30, New International Version).*

However, my ten years of digital marketing experience was entirely secular. I had never done an advertising campaign for a church project before, and consequently prayed a lot in the weeks leading up to the clinic. When the event began I was overjoyed at the testimonies of people who said their family member, friend, or neighbor saw an ad online and told them to come. According to the exit surveys, social media outperformed all the traditional advertising, and was second only to referral by friend or family member. Based on the anecdotal testimonies, word-of-mouth (friend/family) was also largely driven by the social media campaign.

"This took place for two years, so that all who lived in Asia heard the word of the Lord, both Jews and Greeks" (Acts 19:10, NASB).

Social media is the modern School of Tyrannus, a place where the ancient Ephesians gathered to engage with new ideas, pass the time, share thoughts, and participate in discussions. Paul spoke at the School of Tyrannus in Greece for two years (Acts 19:8-9), essentially getting the gospel to go viral in his day.[13]

Paul stayed in one place, and yet his teachings spread. How did this happen?

Ephesus was an important port for trade and commerce (like the internet), attracting people from all over the Roman Empire. People would come and hear what he had to say, go home, and tell others what they'd learned. In today's terminology, they hit "Like" and "Share" on social media, and their friends and family were exposed to Paul's teachings of the gospel. Social media has the potential to do this on a much larger scale. By reaching the connected, we can reach the unreachable.

What starts in the digital space, isn't confined to the digital space.

In other words, if approximately 42% of the world's population is on social media, it's highly likely that they know the other 58% of the world or know someone who is connected to someone who is not on social media. You get the idea.

12 "Social Media and Psychology: 8 Lessons for Marketers." *Hootsuite Social Media Management*, 2 May 2019, blog.hootsuite.com/social-media-psychology/.
13 (Dee Casper, Director, CORE at Pennsylvania Conference of Seventh-day Adventists)

We must put our assumptions about those people aside (whoever those people might be), and work with who we can reach.

Evangelism experts tell me that the best way to reach a community or people group is to empower a member of that community. Your average person is just as likely to have moved several times, as to have lived and died in the community they were born, surrounded by a homogeneous collective of people who share the same culture and life experiences. The "simple life" has given way to something more complicated, perhaps messy. Even for those who never change their geographical location, they are globally connected to people through social media in ways that were unheard of just twenty years ago. What this means is that we now live in a world of intersecting cultures and communities.

> *The city of Ephesus experience is now reflected in every major city in the world and online.*

I, myself, am a mid-western transplant to the D.C. metropolitan area. There is still no cellphone reception in my home town. My parents access the internet and phone through satellite. Until recently, our roads were unpaved, and my family was on well water. I go home once or twice a year and call my parents regularly (when the satellite phone is working). I had never heard of Adventism until I went to college; now my parents are closely connected to two Adventists (me and my husband). During our conversations and interactions, I share my experiences and new ideas. While my home town is not as remote as some other countries or communities that still exist in the world, the concept is the same. We can reach people online who have migrated to the digitally connected parts of the world. These people probably maintain ties to their home communities in some way, and since they are from that community, they are in the best position to share the gospel within the cultural norms, language, and expectations of those communities. When they visit their friends and family, they can share the gospel just like the ancient citizens of the Roman empire did back in the first century.

This is how we can obtain global impact through digital communications. It's the same strategy that Paul leveraged, but scaled up by modern technology.

According to **Pew Research**[14], the most racially diverse Christian denomination in North America is the Seventh-day Adventist Church. We are truly a global movement that has yet to realize the full potential of modern technologies. Our challenge is not to just reach those who are online, but to also activate the online and offline sharing power of those we connect with. The membership of the Adventist Church is perfectly positioned to reach the around the world to every nation, tribe, people, and tongue with the gospel message.

---

14 "The Seventh-Day Adventist Church Is the Most Diverse Church Group in America, Says Study." *The Christian Post*, www.christianpost.com/news/the-seventh-day-adventist-church-is-the-most-diverse-church-group-in-america-says-study.html.

And for those isolated communities with, assumed, no access to the outside world, give the Holy Spirit a little credit for being able to carry the message the rest of the way.

We aren't expected to accomplish this mission alone, but we are called to "Go into all the world and preach the gospel to all creation" (Mark 16:15, NIV). The world now includes the digital space. We need to dream bigger when doing God's work. Can you imagine what would happen if each of us committed to sharing the gospel online for two years? And remember, it's not like we have to physically go somewhere, or even leave the couch for that matter! Who knows where God will lead us when we step out in faith.

If the message went global in Paul's day without the help of modern technology, let's not assume limitations on the Holy Spirit in our day.

Your Audience

The Seeker's Journey

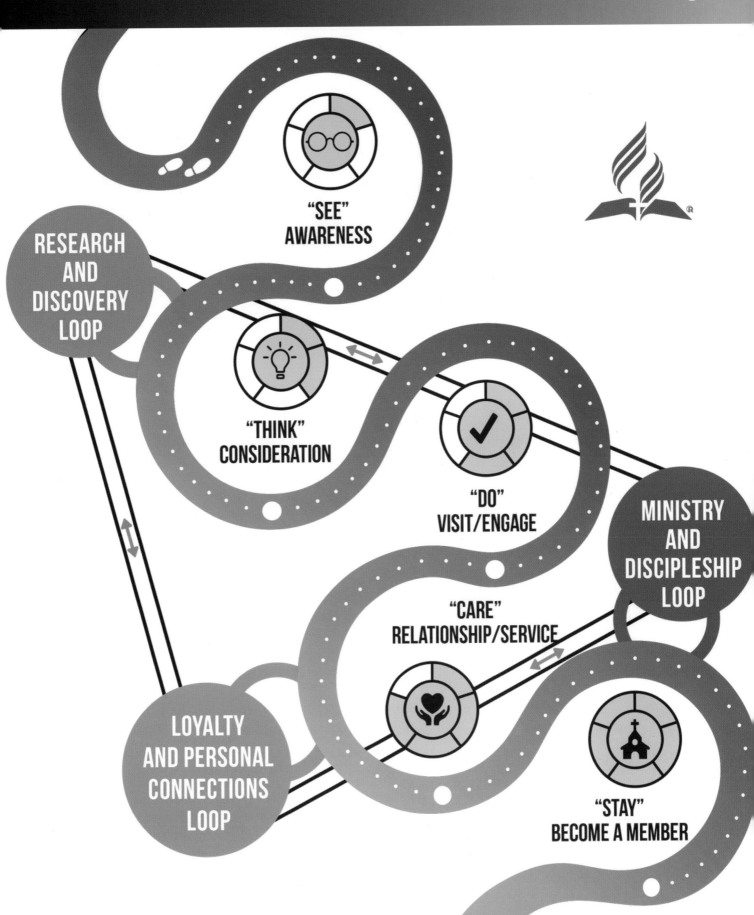

Traditional marketing and evangelism takes a linear approach, starting with attracting "leads" and eventually aiming to convert people into members. While this strategy worked for a long time, the world has changed dramatically in the past few decades. It no longer makes sense, nor is it effective, to group people together into one-size fits all categories and then take a cookie-cutter approach to encouraging spiritual conversion. In addition, the assumptions we make about people groups can often be misleading or even harmful. Therefore, we must fundamentally change the way we approach evangelism.

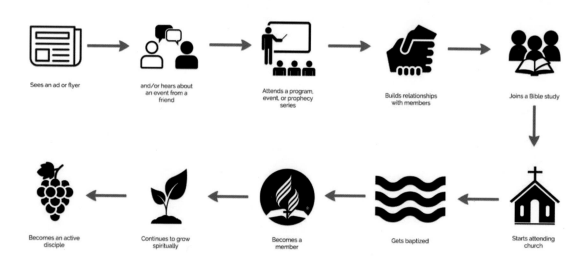

Traditional Marketing/Evangelism
a linear path from attracting "leads" to converting people into members

Sees an ad or flyer — and/or hears about an event from a friend — Attends a program, event, or prophecy series — Builds relationships with members — Joins a Bible study — Starts attending church — Gets baptized — Becomes a member — Continues to grow spiritually — Becomes an active disciple

Credit: Graphic designed by Jamie Domm

Understanding Your Audience

Your average person is just as likely to have moved several times, as to have continuously lived in the community they were born, surrounded by a homogeneous collective of people who share the same culture and life experiences. The "simple life" has given way to something more complicated, and, perhaps, messy. But even for those who have never changed their geographical location, people are now globally connected through social media in ways that were unheard of just 20 years ago. What this means is that we now live in a world of intersecting cultures or communities. These cultures are potentially endless in variety, but we'll unpack a few in the next section on target audiences.

The concept of cultural empathy is well known in the physical mission field. Evangelism experts know that the best way to reach a community or people group is to empower a member of that community to evangelize to their own. Or at the very least, speak the language of the people and show sensitivity and respect to their cultural paradigms. Non-native members of a culture group must sincerely seek to understand the community and reach them where they are in a way that is relevant. We have forgotten this principle when it comes to online evangelism and online communities. While digital evangelism or discipleship is a new concept for the Church, we can remember and apply tried and true bits of wisdom previously uncovered by experienced evangelists and geographically focused missionaries. Digital tools are a way to magnify the reach and impact of traditional and friendship evangelism, not necessarily replacing it. Digital platforms allow us to scale up our efforts in a low-cost way.

The apostle Paul admonishes us to "become all things to all men, that I may by all means save some" (1 Corinthians 9:19-23 NASB 1977). To accomplish this in modern society, our definition of culture needs to be expanded. Many now find themselves between cultures and functioning in multiple online and offline communities simultaneously. The old marketing strategies of putting people in target groups based on a few identifying factors is no longer reflective of reality.

People no longer fit into neat categories based on surface-level descriptors such as location, race, gender, language, and interests. We must connect with audiences on a deeper level based on unifying needs and core values that transcend standard marketing categorizations. Digital tools can enable us to understand the drivers behind the actions, beliefs, concerns, needs, and values of larger groups, better positioning us to serve them in a relevant way. If we can do this, our audiences will be loyal to our Church brand, because we resonate with them at the core of their worldview. We'll unpack how to better reach, understand, and effectively communicate with target audiences in the next few sections of this guide.

To reach younger generations, we must take an integrated and holistic approach that considers the complexities of modern life and relationships. The components of the traditional model are not dead. Many of these steps are still in play; we just have more resources to reach and interact with people in ways that are relevant to their unique situation. Digital communications is a means to amplify our messages and spiritually feed people seven days a week. In other words, the linear model has given way to a multi-faceted process that can start and stop at various points, with many key entry and engagement points. When we take a holistic approach to understanding our audiences better and use this knowledge strategically to combine traditional with digital strategies, we can fish 24/7 in a much larger pond.

The kingdom of God is an all-day, every-day pursuit. His church should be the same online as offline. After all, church is not a program to watch, but a people to be. Success should not be measured by counting people in a building, but, rather, by whether or not we're building a kingdom.

Digital Evangelism Modified Funnel

Another marketing concept we can use to understand the modern process of evangelism is a funnel, where every person is channeled toward the goal which traditionally has been "become a member." While people can enter and engage at different levels of the funnel in multiple ways, movement toward (and beyond) this goal is the basic principle of the funnel model. Every single transition involves an ask, either implied or explicit. With every reduction in the funnel size, there is an implied exit of people. Every person has the option of moving forward down the chain, living at a stage for a period of time, or deciding to leave the process altogether. We must give easy calls-to-action and lead participants in a way that makes moving to the next step a no-brainer. Eventually the goal is for members to become active disciples who then become part of the funnel mechanism as content creators, distributors, or engagers. This is why this modified funnel fans back out at the base and loops back around. The foundation of this marketing paradigm is built on continuous discipleship and integrated strategies, utilizing a wide range of evangelistic strategies.

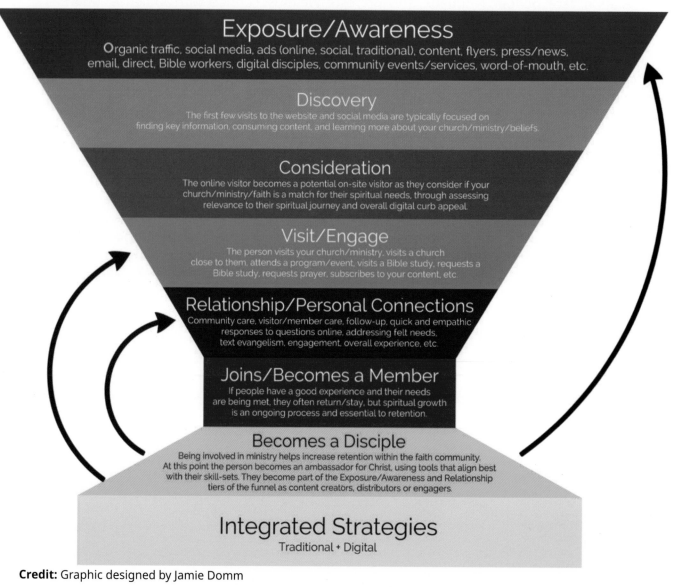

Credit: Graphic designed by Jamie Domm

The Seeker's Journey

To help us better understand how the world of analog and digital experiences interact to move someone through their spiritual journey, we can consider a systems-thinking tool called journey loops.

Systems thinking is a holistic approach to analysis that focuses on the way that a system's constituent parts interrelate and how systems work over time and within the context of larger systems. The systems thinking approach contrasts with traditional analysis, which studies systems by breaking them down into their separate elements... According to systems thinking, system behavior results from the effects of reinforcing and balancing processes" (Margaret Rouse, Techtarget.com). A system is a group of distinct elements that are interrelated and organized to achieve a common purpose or goal.

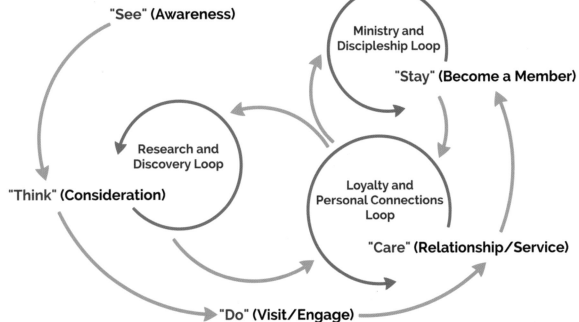

Credit: Graphic designed by Jamie Domm

These steps or loops do not necessarily go in order. A seeker can start at any point, skip sections, leap from loop to loop, and even backtrack. Each loop and experience feeds back into the other steps in the process to help reinforce the journey. I personally started in the "Think" (Consideration) loop, then the "Care" (Relationship/Service) loop and then visited a local church as part of the "Do" (Visit/Engage) loop. This causal loop system is not a perfect representation of the process, but it helps visualize what is actually happening in a complex system or, in this case, journey.

In today's world where people are turning to the internet for answers, the first two parts of the journey are primarily spent in the digital space. Based on the person's situation, they may or may not transition to an in-person experience, though that is always the one of the goals of this process. However, it's important to recognize that experiences in the "Care" and "Stay" loops are just as relevant in the digital space. Therefore, we must seek to find ways to extend the Church experience online, because the in-person experience may not always be possible, at least in the short-term.

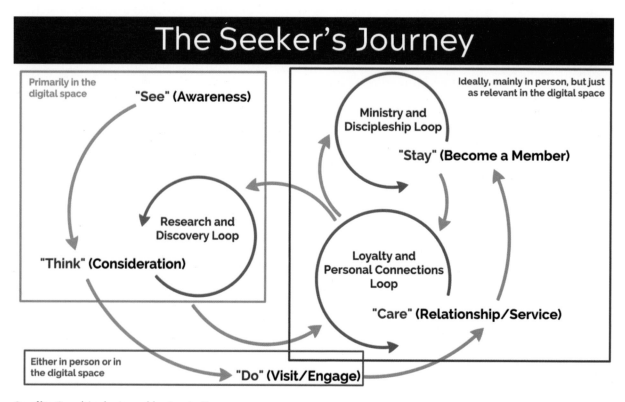

Credit: Graphic designed by Jamie Domm

How the Seeker's Journey fits into the Digital Discipleship and Evangelism Model

Reflecting back on the **Digital Discipleship and Evangelism model**[15], we can see how the three roles or types of digital evangelists can work together to help guide a seeker through a journey of spiritual growth.

Distributors help push out content and messages to help initiate the "See" (Awareness) step and can also function within the "Ministry and Discipleship" loop, using digital tools and technologies to share content within their sphere of digital influence, which, in turn, contributes greatly to the "Research and Discovery" stage.

---

15 "The Digital Discipleship and Evangelism Model." *Digital Evangelism*, www.sdadata.org/digital-evangelism-blog/the-digital-discipleship-and-evangelism-model.

The role of **content creators** is to package the gospel message and teachings of Jesus into various digital-friendly formats, such as: video, blogs, images, podcasts, etc. The resulting content is vital to the growth and decision-making of a seeker within the "Research and Discovery" loop. This content, combined with the role of engagers, can serve as a catalyst to move a seeker to the "Do" (Visit/Engage) and "Stay" (Become a Member) steps.

Engagers are empathic individuals within an organization, or operating independently, who engage in online conversations for the purpose of building meaningful relationships, better understanding needs, and determining meaningful ways to serve others in the community. The engager role spans across multiple touchpoints in the modern seeker's journey and plays a vital role in moving a person towards taking an action and, ultimately, to a faith-based commitment. Social media provides a unique opportunity for long-term member care that can enhance and strengthen the relationships your ministry cultivates with members and the community. We know that connection and relationships is what builds a strong faith community and keeps people in the Church. To that end, engagers are vital to the "Loyalty and Personal Connections" loop as well as the "Do" (Visit/Engage) step and even an integral part of securing a seeker's long-term desire to "Stay" (Become a Member) of a faith community.

Every opportunity to connect is an opportunity to advance the kingdom of God. Our digital voice may be the only opportunity a seeker has to see Christ's love demonstrated in their life. We as a Church should strive to create connections and take a comprehensive approach to facilitating the seeker experience, treating people online as if we're talking with them face-to-face. Their online interactions with you should make them want to experience your faith/mission in person. Then, when they to come for that onsite experience, it should be a continuation of the positive relationship that has been built with them online. There should not be a disconnect between how a person is nurtured in the pews and how they are treated online, or vice-versa.

Understanding Your Target Audience for Effective Communication

You may feel like you know how to use social media platforms for personal sharing, but writing to achieve a marketing/evangelism goal requires much more thought and strategic planning. This section is designed to give you a framework for successfully defining your target audience and determining how to speak to them in a way that is relevant, encouraging meaningful engagements. It is essential that we not only communicate clearly, but that we also take the time to deeply understand our audience. It doesn't matter if you know what you mean. Put yourself in your audience's shoes and speak to them accordingly. Speak to your audience in a way and with the words that enable them to understand and connect with your message. REMEMBER, EMPATHY FIRST.

Good communication is when you communicate in a way your audience understands.

This means that when we communicate in the digital space, we must speak the language of the platform and recognize the "cultural expectations" and "norms" prevalent in the space, as well as within the culture(s) of the people we are communicating to. Without careful research, our words and intentions can easily be taken the wrong way, inadvertently offending and pushing away the very people we are trying to reach.

As Christians, we want to reach and include everyone. This is our ultimate goal as disciples. However, from a specific ministry standpoint, this approach ends up reducing the relevancy of the message and spreads efforts too thin for significant impact. Afterall, a standard marketing rule of thumb states:

If you try to reach everyone all the time, you'll end up
REACHING NO ONE.

Each person, ministry, and local church is uniquely equipped and positioned to reach different types of people. Therefore, it is vital to understand who your audience is before you create content, write a single social media post, or spend any money on social advertisements. This section will help you learn how to effectively shape your messages and content to match your audience's needs and reach them effectively, no matter their age, gender, ethnicity, location, or situation.

Determine Your Target Audience

The first step in reaching your audience is to develop a clear picture of who you are talking to. Begin with surface-level demographic information. Use the space below to fill in the information for your ministry's target audience.

Surface-Level Demographic Information

- Location

_____

- Age

_____

- Gender

_____

- Ethnicity/Language

_____

- Interests

_____

_____

_____

Once you've determined the surface-level characteristics of your target audience, work down to a deeper level which will help shape your messaging and the kind of content you'll create.

Create deep connections by identifying with
CORE VALUES, NEEDS, & COMMON EXPERIENCES.

People no longer fit into neat categories, so we must connect with them on a more profound level, transcending the standard marketing demographics of age, ethnicity, gender, language, location, and interests. If you can dig deeper, your audience will be loyal to your brand because you resonate with them at their core.

The best way to do that is to investigate their needs, experiences, values, and perceptions. Conducting surveys and interviews is one key way to collect more information. Then start asking yourself questions that will help you to get inside the minds of your audience members. What motivates their actions? What makes them who they are? What do they have in common? How can I speak and write in a way that my audience will find relatable? What do they value? What do they actually need?

Examples of needs may include: a spiritually supportive community, affordable education, employment, affordable medical care, safe spaces for their children, mentorship opportunities, a better future, healthier relationships, self-improvement, Christian guidance on real-life issues, food security, or practical life-skills training.

Use the space below to write down possible answers for your target audience.

Deep Level Characteristics

- Needs

  _____

  _____

- Core Values

  _____

  _____

- Shared Experiences

  _____

  _____

- Motivations

  _____

  _____

- Additional Insights

  _____

  _____

"Cultural Empathy" in the Digital Mission Field

As discussed in the previous section, the concept of "cultural empathy" is well known in the physical mission field and its principles should be applied to the digital mission field. We live in a world of intersecting cultures or communities, and, therefore, our definition of culture must expand. Many now find themselves between cultures and functioning in multiple communities simultaneously. In order to identify the unifying threads between seemingly dissimilar people, we need to first unpack their many cultural influences.

These cultures are potentially endless in variety, but can include:
- Platform
- Age groups or generations
- Gender
- Language(s)
- People groups: race, ethnic, immigrant v. first generation, etc.
- Current location: city/suburbs/country
- In school vs. out of school
- Lived in a specific geolocation their whole life vs. transplant
- Faith groups, life-long Adventists vs. converts vs. former Adventists/Christians
- Professional groups vs. homemakers vs. working mothers
- College educated vs. blue-collar workers
- Offline social clubs vs. online identities and groups
- Poverty vs. middle-class vs. wealthy

Use this section to unpack your own intersecting cultures and consider how they may shape your core values and needs.

Now use the following space to write the potential overlap in cultures found within your church, community, ministry, or target audience. How might they influence behavior and needs? What unifying factors can you identify?

_____

_____

_____

_____

_____

_____

_____

_____

Internal vs. External

Are you speaking to Adventists or non-Adventists? Your language may change based on the answer to this question. We must modify the way we communicate in order to effectively reach different audiences without creating barriers. For example, when we are talking to our friends we use certain vernacular that tends to be more playful and friendlier, but when we are talking to our boss or elders, our persona is more serious and professional. The same is true with evangelism and discipleship. We may commonly use certain words such as "Sabbath" or "haystacks" that could seem foreign or confusing to non-Adventists. The list below offers some guidelines on how to distinguish between internal and external audiences.

Internal

- Church members
- Church leaders
- North American Division constituents
- Bible study groups
- Pathfinder/Adventurer participants
- Those raised in the Church/long-time attendees
- Faith communities: city/neighborhoods/ministries

External

- Broader community: neighborhoods/city/state/metro areas
- Businesses
- Related causes or non-profit missions
- Local news

Be careful not to use Adventist-speak when addressing external audiences. Use the space below to indicate who your ministry communicates to on a regular basis, if they are Adventist or non-Adventist, and how you currently interact with them. What changes should you make? What barriers to faith or entry may you be accidentally creating with your words?

_____

_____

_____

_____

_____

_____

Audience Personas 101

When communicating to your audiences, visualize actual people—their interests, culture, wants, needs, and expectations—to refine your voice. You will probably need to create unique personas to represent different target groups within your audience. According to The Guardian, personas can be simply defined as:

"A fictional character that communicates the primary characteristics of a group or segment of your audience and takes into consideration needs, demographics, motivations, and environments."

Determining your audience personas can help you develop and write content that will be relevant and useful to your audience. The best personas are often created by simply talking to your audience, but social media insights, website analytics, and surveys can also prove very useful. Personas give a human face to a collection of information, and they allow you to classify groups for different messaging campaigns and programs. The best personas combine both quantitative and qualitative information.

Below is an example of a persona.

About Bryce: Adventist College Persona
Age: 17
Education: High school senior
Interests: Business, sports, camping, meeting other young people, discipleship training
Salary: $3,000 a year
Location: Berkeley, Calif.
Family: Adopted, married parents, no siblings, Hispanic
Goals: Finding a good paying and meaningful job, mentoring younger peers, finding a girlfriend, finding a Christian friend group

Challenges: Finding friends with similar morals, avoiding drugs/alcohol, food insecure, feels rejected by his biological parents and struggles to connect, struggles with religious doubt

Values: Fair justice system, the environment, good reputation, strong character, fairness, good citizenship, technology and flexibility, diversity, leadership training and experience

Fears: The unknown, poor work-life balance, affording college, student loan debt, getting a good job, rejection, finding purpose/meaning

Preferred platforms for Media: Snapchat, Instagram, YouTube

Messages applicable to Bryce: We are all adopted into God's family. Our church/school/ministry is a place to belong and a place to grow. Connection to others, connection to God. Diversity and purpose. Mentorship opportunities and support for leadership training or education.

Social media personas are developed based on your target audience as defined earlier in this section. The key is finding out what those people want and need; the rest is simply compiling those qualities into a made-up person. As a Church, we need to constantly find ways to reach our audience for the kingdom in the best, most efficient way possible. Creating social media personas is a valuable exercise that enables us, as communicators, to step into others' shoes and view life from their perspective. Personas help us develop empathy with our audience.

Use the following framework to develop your own personas

- Name
- Age/Gender
- Culture/Race/Community
- Education
- Profession
- Income
- Location
- Family Situation
- Faith
- Goals
- Challenges/Needs
- Values
- Fears
- Platforms/Channels for Promotions
- Messages That Would Resonate with Them

Special Note about Generation Z

The Church and the wider Christian community has become increasingly concerned with reaching Generation Z, people born approximately 1997-2012 (Pew Research Center). However, the Church has not yet adapted to meet the needs of the generation before them, Millennials. We should be concerned, as these two age groups represent the largest divergence from traditional Christian values and lowest participation in faith institutions we've seen. To reach and retain these generations, we must reframe our approach based on their perspectives.

Generation Z lives in a totally different world and interacts in a totally different way than any generation before them. When asked what the most important historical event in the USA in the last 20 years was, they responded, "The release of the iPhone." Most older people would say the terrorist attacks of 9/11. (Adam Fenner, Director, *Adventist Learning Community*)

From Gen Z and Millenial perspectives, their answer makes sense given that technology and digital communications have completely reshaped society, how we connect with each other, how we shop, and how we live. They have grown up in an almost entirely digital world, and they relate to technology in a more integrated fashion than any other generation before them.

So who is Gen Z? What you should consider when targeting this age group

- By 2020, people born after 1995 will be **1/3 of the total population in North America** and account for **40% of all US consumers**.
- **It is the most diverse generation** in US history; they don't see diversity unless it's absent.
- **The majority are non-white**, mostly Hispanic.
- 1/10 will marry across racial/ethnic lines.
- 55% prefer to buy clothes online; 53% prefer to buy books and electronics online.
- **They use technology for everything**: grocery shopping, dating, socializing, studying, entertainment, communication, reading the Bible, cooking, etc.
- 70% watch **2+ hours of YouTube a day**.
- **They prefer less public social media** (example: Snapchat).
- Gen Z has an average attention span of 8 seconds; 11% have ADHD.
- **They prefer images, icons, and symbols** (think emojis and gifs) over text.
- **This group is the least religious generation ever**: only 63% are sure God exists; 35% are completely unaffiliated religiously; 28% have never attended a religious service; and 13% are atheist. This may seem discouraging, but it actually shows a huge opportunity if we are willing to meet the challenge.

What are their core values and needs (broadly speaking)?

- 60% want their work to benefit the world.
- 76% are concerned about humanity's impact on the planet.
- They are worried about success, experienced a weak economy early on and have seen the impact of the student loan crisis on Millennials.
- 57% prefer to save over spending (cost-benefit analysis, very pragmatic).
- They interact with media (two-way interactivity) and want it to work from anywhere they are located to fit their lives (example: online education, telecommuting, Uber/Lyft vs. personal vehicles, airBNB vs. hotels).
- They prefer one-on-one social media conversations over lectures.
- They want leadership opportunities.
- They believe in a social gospel: action not words.

Source: Adam Fenner, *Director, Adventist Learning Community*

What do Gen Z's values mean for the Church? It means we must innovate for meaningful impact. If we don't, we only have ourselves to blame for the continuous departures. Change is hard, and the Church is notoriously slow to adapt. Now is the time to act if we really are concerned for the salvation of the next generations. Institutions are not permanent. After all, in the words of W. Edwards Deming, "It is not necessary to change. Survival is not mandatory." The good news is that God never fails. He will always have a people, and He has called us to participate in His great work.

In Summary

We must put our assumptions and judgements in the trash. Too often we create programs and content based on our own interests and passions or based on what we think people need, according to our own perspective and bias. Use the audience factors discussed in this section to make data-informed decisions about your audience, then create programs, messaging, and content based on what you discover. We'll go into content creation in further detail later in the "Content Creators/Creatives" section of this guide. If you're still not sure where to start, spend more time with your target audience and ask more questions. Find out directly from them what they need, what they feel will improve their lives, and what will inspire them to develop a closer relationship with God.

To reach people, we must become a student of their culture. No judgement, only acceptance and adaptation. No one should know more about your audience than you do. Strive to become an expert on the people you are trying to reach.

Speaking to the Collective "We"

To gain insight into the drivers behind the collective shifts in society, read **Pendulum: How Past Generations Shape Our Present and Predict Our Future**, by Roy H. Williams and Michael R. Drew. These shifts impact communication and often drive technology and social change. I recommend that, as part of your efforts to understand how to communicate more effectively to your target audiences and fulfill their needs, you not only read and study this book, but also invest the time in reading **Generations: The History of America's Future, 1584 to 2069** by William Strauss and Neil Howe. Good communication requires speaking in a way our audience can appreciate. As a religious organization, we should be using digital technologies to fulfill our audiences' needs, but to do that, we must first understand what those needs are (as discussed in the previous section), their unspoken expectations, and the forces for change that influence a generation. This section takes the 30,000-foot-view of broader trends that may also be acting upon your target audiences.

Generation Z and the Millennials have been leaving the Church at alarming rates; could it be that we simply don't understand them? We know that people of any given cultural group are always the best suited to reach out and evangelize to their peers. I contend that the same is true with generations. Now, empowering and training members of the youth to reach their own does not permit us to abdicate our function as guides and mentors. We too must seek to understand and cultivate these relationships if we are to bridge the gap and secure the future of the Church in North America and promote the salvation of souls. *Pendulum* provides an analysis of the current shifts in society and their impact on marketing, technology, and communication. The Social Media + Big Data department of the North American Division has repeatedly used these techniques across a broad range of messaging campaigns, consistently yielding successful results. Even if you don't have time to read the 200-page book, what follows is a summary of what you need to know to understand and utilize these communication techniques.

> *"What has been will be again, what has been done will be done again; there is nothing new under the sun. Is there anything of which one can say, 'Look! This is something new'? It was here already, long ago; it was here before our time. No one remembers the former generations, and even those yet to come will not be remembered by those who follow them."* — Ecclesiastes 1:9-11 NIV

Pendulum takes Strauss and Howe's four "generations" (Idealist, Reactive, Civic, Adaptive) and reduces it to two generations covering forty years that oscillate between the "Me" philosophy of individuality, freedom, uniqueness, and potential (peaked in 1983) to the collective "We," working together for the common good, fixing society's greatest problems, and adopting a philosophy of authenticity and transparency. Sound familiar? According to this model, we are currently in the upswing of the "We" that should reach its zenith in 2023. Both ideals are always present in society but shifts in dominance occur. Optimal balance is found between the two extremes, and either extreme has negative consequences.

The main point is that group behavior is predictable, and we can use this predictability to speak to the masses in a relevant way.

There will always be exceptions, and as the authors point out:

- There is always a counterculture within a prevailing culture.
- Individuals are not predictable.

To communicate, we must ask, "What is driving the actions and attitudes of the group?"

"The *Pendulum* predicts only the momentum and direction of the majority in a society—most of the people, most of the time. Certainly not everyone, and certainly not always" (Williams 25). For deeper insight into the pros and cons of each swing of the "pendulum," read the book.

Determine how your mission, programs, product and/or message fits or can be positioned into this paradigm. You may need to reevaluate what your ministry offers to better align with what is relevant to your target audience. See the previous section on understanding your target audience.

Drivers of a "WE" vs. drivers of a "ME"

WE "I'M O.K. YOU'RE NOT O.K." (Witch Hunt)		ME I'M NOT O.K. YOU'RE O.K. (Hero Worship)
• Demands conformity for the common good • Applauds personal responsibility • Believes a million men are wiser than one man (think Wikipedia) • Wants to create a better world: "I came, I saw, I concurred." • Is about small actions • Desires to be part of a productive team • Admires humility and thoughtful persons • Believes leadership is, "This is the problem as I see it. Let's solve it together." • Strengthens society's sense of purpose, focuses on solving problems (antiheroes)		• Demands freedom of expression • Applauds personal liberty • Wants to achieve a better life: "I came, I saw, I conquered." • Is about big dreams • Desires to be number one • Admires individual confidence and decisive persons • Believes leadership is, "Look at me. Admire me. Emulate me if you can." • Strengthens society's sense of identity, elevates attractive heroes

Values and beliefs that motivate society in "WE" and "ME" cycles (Williams 17)

This shift can be seen in successful advertising campaigns that target a worldview/attitude instead of an age group.

In other words, instead of targeting people based on surface level demographics, they are speaking to a shared value that transcends age and race as discussed in the previous section.

In *Pendulum*, the authors point out a well-known example. "Remember L'Oréal's famous '**Me**' slogan, 'Because **I'm** worth it?' As society passed the tipping point of 2003 and the 'Me' became fully unwound, the old slogan was replaced with, 'Because you're worth it'" (Williams 172).

During this same period, the successful Army slogan "Be All You Can Be" (1980-2001) changed to "Army of One" (2001-2006) but didn't perform well because it was "contrary to the idea of teamwork" said Frank Luntz, American political consultant, pollster, and public opinion guru (Ball). The current, more "WE" focused, slogan is "Army Strong."

WE	
TIPS TO CREATE A SERIOUS INTERNET PRESENCE IN A "WE" CYCLE	
• Informative content is the jumbo jet that will take you where you want to go. • The web is an information delivery system, not an advertising vehicle. • Use your site to build confidence, inform your customer (audience/member), and anticipate and answer questions—24/7. • Insightful website architecture and exceptional writing trump dazzling graphics. • Make it easy on your customers (audience/member). Frustrate them and they're gone.	

Mindset and values in society during a "WE" cycle (Williams 168)

Social media is a powerful tool for member care and service[16]. Never before has "truth in advertising" been so important. The younger generations are the most connected, more than any before them, and they naturally turn to social media to voice their displeasure with a brand or experience.

"Your advertising [messaging] may fool one of us. But that one will tell the rest of us," says Roy H. Williams (172).

WE	
UPSWING INTO "WE"	
VALUES	REJECTS
• Authenticity • Teamwork • Humility • Small actions • Personal responsibility • Cold, hard truth	• Hype • Posing • Arrogance • Wishful thinking • Self-righteousness • Sugar-coated nonsense*

Tips to create a serious Internet presence during a "WE" cycle (Williams 172)

* This line was edited for our audience.

"We want the truth, even if it's ugly. Shrink-wrapped, sugar-coated, phony posing [of the 80's through mid-90's] is no longer acceptable" (Williams 163). Humility, straight talk, and a genuine point of view is what the Adventist Church and its ministries need to embrace; we see the effectiveness of this strategy in the success of initiatives like Gorgeous2God. Gorgeous2God is a **community** of young Christian women tackling **real issues** from a godly perspective. True stories from the experiences of real girls are shared and communicated in a candid way that the Church has not embraced previously. Topics include rape, self-harm, sex before marriage, depression, abuse, and other "uncomfortable" topics. Recognizing the underlying cultural principles in a "WE" generation provides guidance and strengthens our abilities to reach our target audience with relevant content, increasing meaningful impact. As a result of continued audience-focused messaging and content development, Gorgeous2God has grown to over 45K followers on social media, with over 20K visitors to the website a year, countless interactions and hundreds of direct messages (as of July 2019).

> *"Self-effacing transparency is utterly disarming."*
> —Michael R. Drew

Analyze your audience; consider the factors discussed in this section and the previous section to then shape your communications in a way that aligns with the drivers behind the current (broad) shifts in society. Position your ministry for success. You will always have outliers within your target audience, but utilizing this knowledge allows your ministry to fish more effectively and increases the potential for a larger catch.

Sources

Ball, Molly (January 6, 2014) "The Agony of Frank Luntz." *The Atlantic*.

Williams, R.H., & Drew, M. R. (2012). Pendulum: how past generations shape our present and predict our future. New York: Vanguard Press.

Tools and Resources

What are Digital Tools
& Why are They Important

If you feel that you have a solid grasp of what modern communication tools and technologies are, you may want to skip down to the second part of this section. However, we felt it appropriate to include a general description to ensure a common understanding among a diverse audience. For the purposes of digital discipleship and evangelism, let's define digital tools and technologies as: devices, web-based platforms, applications, and software that process and use information (videos, text, images etc. in numerical form known as binary code) to communicate or connect with other devices and software through the internet or with cellular data. More simply put, these are devices and web-based tools that enable individuals to share ideas, communicate to a global audience, and connect with people anywhere almost instantaneously.

These tools encompass a wide variety of technologies that many people interact with daily and include, but are not limited to:

- Social media and content-sharing platforms
- Email
- Websites/blogs
- Podcasts
- Digital advertising (outdoor signage, sponsored social media posts or website sidebars, for example)
- Instant messaging/chat widgets
- Texting
- Smart phones
- Business review platforms
- Digital meeting and video conferencing tools
- Digital cameras
- Smart phone applications
- Computer applications and programs (Microsoft Word, Spotify, Google Chrome, etc.)
- Search Engine Optimization
- Computers and tablets
- Smart TVs

Connecting with the Local Community

Digital tools have become an integral part of the fabric of modern living, but as a Church, we have yet to fully tap into their potential for sharing the gospel and directly serving our communities. As discussed previously, people spend significantly more time socializing online than they do in person. Social media and other digital communication tools allow us to not only go global, but effectively reach and permeate our local communities with positive messages and mission projects.

When we think of missionaries, we usually think of traveling to far away lands and learning new languages in order to communicate. However, what is becoming ever clearer for the Church in North America is that our biggest challenge is reaching our local neighbors in an increasingly post-modern, secular society.

The mission field is right next door, and it's just as legitimate.

Digital technologies have made it easier than ever to:

- get to know the needs of our community
- let people know they are heard and understood
- connect with our neighbors
- build relationships
- let them know we're here to help

With digital tools, we can accomplish these objectives quickly and implement them on a large scale for a relatively low cost—empowering churches to become more than the building up the street, but rather an active and engaged people who benefit the larger community through their care and relevant acts of service. A common expression says, "People don't care how much you know, until they know how much you care." We can and should be attending to people's felt needs first, then inviting them to follow Christ after we've already developed a friendly and trusting relationship.

The most meaningful expression of our mission of hope and wholeness is in the context of the local church.

The potential of digital evangelism and discipleship must be realized at the individual church level. A top-down approach cannot meet the needs of your neighbors, but you and your congregation can. The Adventist Church began as a grassroots movement, and we can re-embrace this mentality to reach the modern seeker next door. With over 1.2 million Adventists in the North American Division and over 5,500 churches, there is a lot of untapped potential.

The true power of the local church is in its unique ability to create and sustain meaningful relationships with people. Social media and other digital technologies are merely tools that can be used to scale up these efforts beyond who we physically meet. They can also assist us in being more targeted and relevant in our approach to evangelism, by revealing the felt needs and demonstrated behaviors of our community. I believe that the next great awakening in North America will be a digital one, but we must work intentionally where we are, in order to more effectively reach people where they are in their spiritual journey. In the following sections we'll expound upon this principle, mapping out practical ways to leverage digital discipleship and evangelism.

Who is Part of the Digital Discipleship & Evangelism Team?

In terms of who makes up the digital discipleship and evangelism team, our philosophy includes *everyone*. The integrated model utilizes every active member in a holistic approach that aims to *scale up* the traditional friend/community evangelism and discipleship models, not replace them.

What does this mean practically?

It's not a digital approach attempting to subvert a traditional approach, but, rather, the entire church body using all its human resources, diversity of spiritual gifts, and available tools to work together for a common goal. Church growth is a product of promotion, experience, and personal connections. Digital technology is a powerful tool to guide more people into your church, but the on-site experience and personal connections is what will keep them coming. After all, it's one challenge to attract new people; it's another to get them to keep returning. To encourage people to remain in your community, whether online or in person, they must not only have a good experience, but also connect with the members on a personal level and become integrated as a participating member of the community.

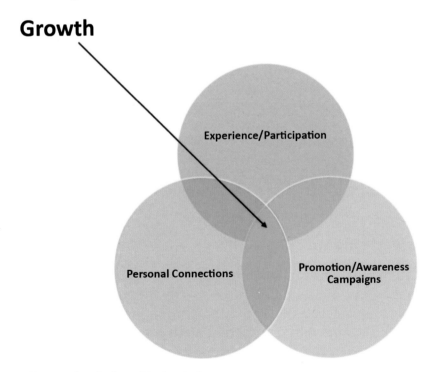

Credit: Graphic designed by Jamie Domm

If we understand the local church to be a community of believers, we must seek to create meaningful connections, reaching out to seekers whose experience often starts online, as well as to those already in our house of worship. Your church's online interactions with potential visitors should make them want to experience your faith and mission in person. Then, when they do come for that on-site experience, it should be a continuation of the positive relationship you've built with them online. The same is true in reverse.

To achieve a continuity of experience and relationship building, everyone is part of the process. This means the 84-year-old greeter at the door is part of your digital discipleship and evangelism team just as much as the tech savvy youths who create video snippets and content for your social media. It includes the passionate and knowledgeable worship leaders who answer questions and host online bible studies. Remember, what starts in the digital space is not confined to the digital space. It may take weeks, months, or years, but eventually those people who have been touched by your digital voice may be moved by the Holy Spirit to walk in the door. From their perspective, it's all one spiritual journey and experience, not digital versus traditional. They don't view their experience in silos; therefore, we must break down the silos of how we go about discipleship and evangelism.

Every touchpoint matters and must tell a consistent story!

Look at this process of evangelism holistically. Consider all possible touchpoints in the list below and ask, "Where does the experience decelerate? Where is the breakdown in communication?"

Touchpoints by role groupings include but are not limited to:

Creatives/Creators

Traditional: outreach materials, presentations, events, classes, seminars, wearables/flare, ephemera, print/radio advertising, direct mail pieces, billboards, flyers, bulletins, print newsletters, print publications/literature, other handouts, signage, posters, branded vehicles, letterhead, business cards, general resources, radio ministry

Digital: digital advertising messages and design, digital newsletters/emails, digital publications/blogs, digital flyers, website(s), social media content, videos, online resources, podcasts

Engagers (Experience and Relationship Building)

Traditional: telephone, voicemail, services to community/members, small groups, ministries, classes, seminars, events, Bible studies, resources (access to people and print materials), children's programs, fellowship meals, prayer groups, mentorship, worship experience on site, interactions with members, church culture and environment, customer service (aka people care), greeters, parking, follow-up, personal connections

Digital: website(s), chat tools, social media conversations, videos, AV, IT, texting, resources (access to people and digital literature), worship experience online, live-streaming, video content, customer service (aka people care), follow-up, personal connections, interactions with members through digital tools, online community culture, video conferencing, online Bible studies

Distributors

Traditional: outreach efforts, Bible workers, door knocking, public relations, word of mouth, wearables/flare, ephemera, print/radio advertising, direct mail, billboards, flyers, bulletins, print newsletters, other handouts, signage, posters, branded vehicles

Digital: outreach efforts, digital Bible workers, digital door knocking, word of mouth, digital communications, online public relations, digital advertising, digital flyers, digital newsletters/emails, AV, IT, texting, social media posts/invites, social media ambassadors, live-streaming, video conferencing.

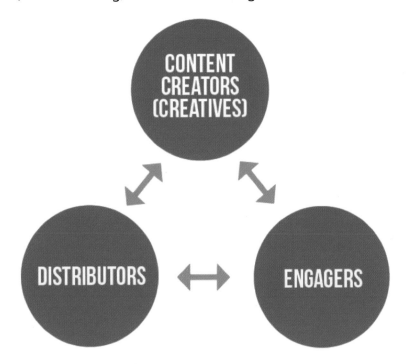

Credit: Graphic designed by Brittany McNitt

With the digital discipleship and evangelism model shown above as a foundational concept, we can understand how the roles of creators, distributors, and engagers can fit into the overall seeker/visitor experience.

There may be an overlapping of functions that can occur at multiple touchpoints. Every church is different and has different human resources, and spiritual gifts to draw from. This concept is scalable and adaptable to your situation.

Make room for digital discipleship and evangelism

Change can be difficult, especially for institutions grounded in tradition. However, the Adventist Church is also rooted in a movement that was led by young people. We must again empower talented youths in our churches to take the lead in areas where they naturally excel, such as digital communications and community building. In addition, we have not done a good job of recognizing and utilizing the spiritual gifts of tech savvy and creative members. These gifted individuals have a wealth of talent to offer mission work and should be encouraged to use their skills in service. We can change the culture in our faith communities to make them feel that the Church truly values their time and talents just as much as Bible workers, nurses, Bible study leaders, and speakers.

Form teams of content creators, distributors, and engagers. Each church likely has various members who could specialize or lead in certain areas. These can be powerful personal ministry opportunities, especially for empathetic persons who can facilitate positive conversations online and share stories of faith. Seek to create a culture of sharing and engaging with church social media content as a means for individuals to help fulfill the church's mission and expand the reach of messages. Anyone who is on social media, has an email address, or is connected to the internet can share content.

It doesn't matter if a person has four friends or 40,000, they have influence.

Find ways to leverage social influence. If people are connected to others through digital technologies, they have digital influence. Each impression/message received represents a person touched by your message and mission. "Social butterflies" can learn to use their online and offline influence to engage in practical mission work. There is a place for all skill levels.

Influencer groups in your church may include, but are not limited to:

- Choir and music ministry groups
- Prayer groups
- Bible study groups
- AV/IT
- Greeters
- Social butterflies
- Hospitality team
- Personal ministries
- Administration
- Pastors
- Youth leaders

- Designers
- Creatives
- Videographers
- Writers
- Techies
- Marketers/communicators
- Community outreach leaders
- Bible workers
- Health professionals
- Any other groups or ministries

We'll explore in depth the roles and their scope of work within the digital discipleship and evangelism model later in this guidebook.

Organize multi-generational training and mentorship opportunities. This will only strengthen your church body and improve cross-generational relationships. Young people yearn for mentorship, and the older generations can learn a lot form the natural skills of the youth. The church should be the ideal example of two-way mentorship in action. Ultimately technologies change, but people and their needs largely remain the same. Healthy communities involve multiple generations coexisting in a collaborative and supportive manner.

In summary, to make room for digital discipleship and evangelism in your church:

- **Empower the tech savvy and creative members of your church**; make them feel that the church values their time and talents.
- **Create personal ministry opportunities**; train empathic people to engage in conversations online and to become content creators.
- **Create a culture of digital sharing and content engagement.**
- **Utilize and empower digital influencers and social butterflies.**
- **Set up training sessions and opportunities for two-way mentorship.**

Utilize Digital Bible Workers

If you are lucky enough to have a Bible worker, empower them to expand their efforts digitally. Social media and other digital technologies can be leveraged as lead generating tools. Remember, young people spend upwards of 9-18 hours a day behind a screen, and that affords the church a lot of opportunities to reach them with relevant content and conversations facilitated for seekers. Ideally this is someone who can ultimately lead a focused evangelistic effort, train others, build a dedicated team, and work with other groups and initiatives within your church.

Digital technologies allow a Bible worker to enter a person's life at the convenience and comfort level of the recipient by providing relevant online content, a degree of anonymity, a simple platform for question and answers, and opportunities to engage and form relationships.

What does a Digital Bible Worker Do?

Digital Bible workers utilize digital technologies to share the gospel and stimulate religious thought by creating and packaging content that addresses relevant needs/ questions and encourages people to advance in their spiritual journey. Digital Bible workers build relationships with those in the broader community, online and offline, and usually within a specific geographic territory in order to create opportunities for one-on-one or small group Bibles studies held in person or via digital tools. They work in partnership with a local church and pastor to evaluate the needs of a community and determine relevant opportunities for outreach and service. They mentor converts in their development of Christian character and commitment to faith as well as train and equip new members for active discipleship roles. This role encompasses a mix of digital discipleship and evangelism to bridge the gap between working in the digital mission field and achieving real-world impact.

The following is sample of what a job description could look like for local churches and conferences looking to hire a Bible worker to lead online evangelistic campaigns. This position can also be adapted to more appropriately reflect the role of a digital pastor. Feel free to adapt to your specific needs and HR requirements. View this template as a type of menu to guide you in the creation of a position that makes sense for your organization's structure. These positions can be adapted for paid or volunteer workers based on the level of time commitment needed and budget available.

Position Summary

The Digital Bible Worker will implement a comprehensive, multi-channel digital evangelism strategy designed to meet the spiritual and social needs of teen, 18– to 35-year-old, collegiate, career-focused, single or married seekers (may include other target audiences based on the goals of the conference or church) in the local community. While engagement and relationship building will start in the digital space, the intent is to bring the target audience to an in-person experience. A secondary goal of this position is to mentor young people already in the church towards a deeper relationship with Jesus and greater community involvement—empowering them to also be effective digital disciples.

Objectives and Responsibilities

Essential Job Functions

- Work closely with a pastor, congregation or conference to utilize digital technologies for the purpose of achieving the organization's goals.

- Implement a comprehensive, multi-channel digital evangelism strategy designed to build relationships with the local users of social media platforms. The strategy should also meet the spiritual and social needs of teen, 18- to 35-year-old, collegiate, career-focused, single, and married truth seekers or other target audiences based on the over-arching goals of the church or conference.

- Plan and implement a monthly content calendar for weekly video devotionals on appropriate social media platforms. Write, film, edit, and upload weekly devotionals. Respond to comments and build community on social media platforms through digital evangelism.

- Develop and manage an advertising budget and set goals to promote devotionals and local fellowship opportunities on Facebook, Instagram, and other media as necessary. The purpose of this advertising would be to raise awareness, attract youth to engage with relevant content, and encourage relationship building that starts in the digital space and migrates to in-person interactions.

- Use momentum from video devotionals to move into a longer format online Bible discussion/study that acts as a weekly livestreamed "Branch Sabbath School," with live, interactive audience participation to further foster community engagement. The goal is to encourage open and honest conversations to equip youth to stand for their faith in a post-modern world.
- Obtain Bible study interest contacts through digital engagements and social media ad promotions. Respond in a timely matter to all messages and questions posted online.
- Participate in available continuing education sessions on evangelism offered by the local conference and digital communication training opportunities available online.

Traditional Ministry

- Provide guidance and support based on biblical principles to young adults in an honest and open manner. Speak to young adults who desire authenticity, while using the anonymity of the digital space to engage privately when needed.
- Plan monthly, in-person young adult meet-ups (advertised online, through partner churches, email, and social media).
- Work with the conference to promote young adult events.
- Offer one-on-one Bible studies as requested, in person and digitally, using free video conference tools.

Leadership

- Train and mentor other young adults to lead in ministry both in person and in the digital space. Equip them to give Bible studies, lead outreach, and get involved in ministry by utilizing digital technologies, empowering them to become digital disciples.
- Provide church-wide visibility and communication about young adult activities.
- Participate on the church leadership team.
- Identify, develop, and implement solutions to strategically meet the needs of young people in collaboration with established youth and young adult ministries.
- Have regular meetings with the pastor or the pastoral staff to report results, as well as give a full report during each board meeting.

Education and Experience

- Bachelor's degree (BA/BS) or master's degree preferred. Religion-related field preferred. Relevant work experience may be considered in lieu of educational requirements.
- 2-5 years experience in youth/young adult ministry preferred.
- Demonstrated mature and growing faith in Jesus Christ.

- Extensive knowledge of principles, policies and beliefs of the Seventh-day Adventist Church and North American Division of the General Conference. This includes knowledge of Church structure and committee procedures.
- Excellent interpersonal skills with strong relationship-building mindset.
- Knowledge and skill in appropriate methods of dealing with human behavior in various circumstances and from different backgrounds.
- Demonstrated strong leadership skills.
- Biblical teaching and preaching ability.
- Moderate to advanced computer and digital communication skills to facilitate ministry activities.
- Basic to moderate understanding of integrated (traditional + digital) marketing strategies and promotion.
- Basic to moderate understanding of video software and editing tools as well as the ability to communicate ideas on camera in an engaging and clear manner.
- Willingness to learn new skills and ability to adapt to changes in digital technology.
- Must be a committed Seventh-day Adventist in good standing with the Church, including regular church attendance, participation, and involvement as well as demonstrated faithfulness in stewardship as understood by the Church and adherence to the Church standards as defined by the Church manual.

The Basics
of Strategy

BEST PRACTICE

It All Begins with a Strong Foundation

I occasionally receive criticism online from believers who think I need to be reminded that Jesus is our rock, not worldly marketing best practices. However, understanding that any missionary effort must have its foundation in Christ does not negate our responsibility to educate ourselves in the most effective ways to reach people with the tools available. I have witnessed far too many situations where well-meaning people fly by the seat of their pants, don't plan appropriately, leave all the details to Jesus, and pray everything works out okay. As a result, the impact of the event or campaign is not what it could have been. Think how much more effective we could be if we practiced good stewardship through proper organization, planning, and communication best practices. The Bible teaches us that a strong foundation is important, both for personal spiritual health as well as for effective witnessing. We should take this wisdom seriously and do everything we can to share the gospel effectively, leaving what we cannot do to the Holy Spirit. A wise person once said:

Don't pray for the things you can or should do yourself.
Ask God for the things only He can do.

A Strong Foundation Begins with Leadership

Whether you're a ministry, church, conference, or independent missionary, here is what leaders can start doing today to build a strong strategic foundation for sharing your ministry message:

- Include digital strategies in short- and long-term visions and goals.
- Dedicate funds for social media promotions.
- Dedicate time for training you and your staff.
- Identify staff who could take on social media as part of their job duties (*this may mean taking something else off their plate*).
- Invest in young people; give them space to utilize their skills in this area for the Church.
- Take advantage of all our free resources, classes, and case studies on **SDAdata.org**.

The stakes of our gospel calling are too high; your church, conference, or ministry can no longer go without a digital strategy. It is imperative that we become just as effective as secular organizations at using digital media for communication and community building.

Social Media & Digital Communications Audit

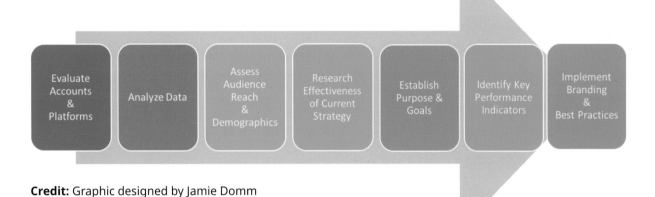

Credit: Graphic designed by Jamie Domm

Begin by evaluating your existing accounts and platforms. Ask: "Are we using the right ones for our audience and mission?" and "Are there opportunities for consolidation?"

Strategic planning is simply the process of being intentional and thoughtful with your digital communications.

Less is more. When you streamline your communication efforts, you will achieve greater impact.

Look at your data to determine who you are reaching, the effectiveness of your current strategy, and areas for best practice implementation. Look for issues with your foundation and start thinking about digital strategy goals, target audiences, and key metrics.

Define your purpose for being on social media and utilizing digital tools. Then frame your strategy accordingly, identifying key performance indicators for success.

Many ministries and churches fall into the trap of reactive digital communications versus proactive. Reshape your strategy so that you are ahead of the ball. Develop and implement branding guidelines for all your digital communications (which should be an extension of your traditional media, like print) and make sure your team follows best practices.

Understanding Purpose

Start a Conversation	Make Connections	Break Down Barriers	Influence Network	Advance the Gospel
•Friendly •Human •Approachable •Sincere •Non-judgemental	•Connect to God •Connect with others •Connect others to gospel	•Open communication •Listen •Restore relationships	•Calls to action •Get involved •Connect/Follow •Share content •Invite others	•Grow God's kingdom •Encourage social media ambassadors •Serve the community

Credit: *Heidi Baumgartner, edited by Jamie Domm*

The auditing process should help you evaluate your current system of communication and develop clear objectives for your digital communications, such as: to advance the gospel and positively influence your community. You and your team can then develop an ongoing approach that aims to achieve some of the key areas listed above.

Setting Goals

Once you have a purpose, you can set goals. When you know what you are trying to achieve, you can set benchmarks for measurement. Then came up with a strategy and budget.

Examples of some goals may include, but are not limited to:

Increase fan base and drive traffic to the website.

Increase event attendance & participation.

Increase community awareness to become more than a building up the street.

Get to know your membership/community better and understand their felt needs.

Encourage social media ambassadors to share your content and invite people to your events.

Increase meaningful engagement online.

Develop digital disciples who actively share their faith in the digital space.

Reach target groups with meaningful content.

Improve the lives of others.

Communicate core values.

Create connection and foster relationships.

Define why you are unique, becoming a resource to the community.

Set expectations, both for those who interact with you and for your team.

Create clarity and focus. When everyone on your team (whether that's a few people or an entire church) understands what they are trying to achieve, it enables them to find their place within your mission.

Performance Metrics (aka Key Performance Indicators)

Once you've identified why you'll be using digital media and who you're trying to reach, it's important to implement measures for success. Identify the metrics that are the most important for your goals and decide how to track them. If you don't have a lot of time, set benchmarks and track high-level numbers.

Types of Digital/Social Media Metrics

Activity metrics: quantity of posts and content created (a great metric for beginners who are starting a content strategy from scratch)

Reach metrics: number of people who see your content and their demographic data

Engagement metrics: interactions and interest in your brand and content

Acquisition metrics: changes in engagement over time or "relationships developed"

Conversion metrics: actions, sales, registrations, resource requests, and other results

Retention metrics: happy customers and brand evangelists

Source: Buffer[17], *edited by Jamie Domm*

For example, key performance indicators for ministry could include, but are not limited to

Activity metrics: number of videos/podcasts/new content created by the team.

Reach metrics: reach/impressions/views for your content in general or from a specific age group, location, or people group. Also, traffic to the website in general or from a specific channel, platform, or location.

Engagement metrics: quantity of followers, likes, shares, comments, or messages.

Acquisition metrics: empowerment of social media ambassadors and the resulting activity, number of questions submitted, active online Bible studies, Bible study requests, or active (ongoing) conversations.

Conversion metrics: number of volunteers, registration numbers, event attendance, donations, visits to the church, quantity of purchases, baptisms, one-on-one meetings, as well as book, Bible study, and resource requests.

Retention metrics: testimonials, repeated visitors to your church, positive impressions shared, people sharing their experience with their online friends/followers, meeting felt needs, developing a presence in the community, increased involvement in ministry.

Choosing the Right Platforms/Channels

Remember, to reach your target audience, you must go to where they spend their time online and use the language they use. Refer back to the **"Understanding Your Target Audience"**[18] section to help identify the best platforms for your chosen target audience(s). It's very easy to become overwhelmed by all the possibilities. To avoid that, start with just

---

17 Seiter, Courtney. "61 Social Media Metrics, Defined." Buffer Marketing Library, *Buffer Social Blog*, 30 Nov. 2018, buffer.com/library/social-media-metrics.

18 "Understanding Your Target Audience for Effective Communication." *Digital Evangelism*, www.sdadata.org/digital-evangelism-blog/understanding-your-target-audience-for-effective-communication.

a few platforms that make the most sense for your ministry, your messages, your available human resources, and your goals. It's best to pick a few platforms and do them well! A strategy that is stretched too thin will not get the results you're hoping for.

Remember the "Rule of 7"

The "Rule of 7" states that a person needs to be exposed to a message at least seven times before they will take a desired action, such as register, RSVP, attend an event, request a resource, send a message, read an article, or participate in some other meaningful way.

Everyone, including our audience, experiences marketing messaging and content overload. It's estimated that the average adult is exposed to over 3,000 marketing messages a day! Therein lies the challenge. To cut through the clutter, we must utilize a multi-channel, multi-platform approach. Also, consistency with your branding, as well a regular messaging schedule, will maximize effectiveness. Channel typically refers to the communication medium, such as radio, print, TV, or social media. Platform refers to different kinds of social media such as Facebook, Snapchat, YouTube, and Instagram. Truly effective communication strategies work across all channels and platforms to reach people where they are, conveying one consistent goal or message.

This is often referred to as integrated marketing and may utilize the following channels:

- Print
- Email
- Social media
- Radio
- Television
- Text messages
- Websites

Social media should be part of a comprehensive communication strategy that incorporates both traditional media and digital, working together to maximize impact. In most cases, social media is not used in place of traditional forms of communication, but in addition, as a means of amplifying your message to a larger community.

For churches, you'll most likely want to leverage in-person interactions and conversations, website updates, text messages, flyers, group messaging tools, podium announcements, emails, and your social media profiles. Together, all these efforts help communicate your church brand, and it's important to consider how each of these communication tools reflects your message, mission, and, ultimately, Christ, following His example for drawing people to the gospel. Being strategic is just being intentional with how you orchestrate all the different ways to distribute information, and making sure to use effective methods of presenting that information. If you find yourself struggling to make your members informed about events and opportunities, understanding and implementing this multi-channel principle will help improve awareness amongst your congregation.

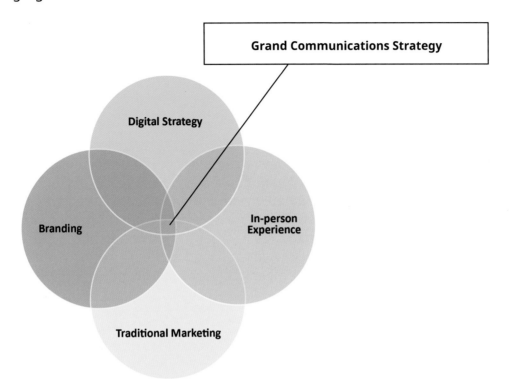

Credit: Graphic designed by Jamie Domm

But with the busyness of life, how can you ensure that your audience prioritizes your messages? Your content must be read before it can have any kind of life-changing effect. It's not enough to communicate often and in different ways. To stand out and be effective, your messages should communicate directly to the reader in a way that is relevant to their life or situation, framed in a way that meets their needs. Messaging like: "This will make your life easier/help you with a problem," or "Here's a chance to learn how to eat healthier/ help the community," or "Here's an opportunity to gain some insight on that nagging question you have," is strong, engaging content.

Another way to think about this is to seek to understand the motivating desires and core values of your community. Refer back to the **"Understanding Your Target Audience"**[19] section of this guide for more information on this topic. Then create programs, ministries, and content that serves them. Too often we create the programs and content that we assume our audience wants, and don't end up with the results we were hoping for. When we combine a strong communications strategy with careful research about our target audience prior to creating programs and messages, we can increase our chances of being successful. We'll unpack messaging and content more under the "Content Creators" section of this guide.

Implementing an effective strategy requires repeated, consistent messaging from multiple communication channels to have an informed audience or membership. In addition, those messages must serve your target audiences in a meaningful way. We now have more resources than ever before to reach audiences and reinforce our message. But with all the digital clutter, it might take up to a thousand tries to reach someone just seven times! Therefore, it's important to keep at it and develop relationships with those you are trying to serve.

Get Organized

Social media can seem daunting, but it doesn't have to be. For most Adventist entities, communications manager is just one of many hats an employee might wear—especially if you are a small team or just a team of one. If you happen to be a full-time digital strategist, you're likely managing multiple campaigns and projects at once. Regardless of your level of expertise and available resources, there never seems to be enough time in the day to accomplish everything you need to do in order to stay on top of the ever-growing evangelistic influence of digital media. A streamlined approach allows you and your team to tackle multiple projects that must integrate an ever-growing list of communication channels.

We'll unpack the details of a content strategy within the "Content Creators" section of this guidebook. For now, here are some fundamental tips for getting organized:

- **Develop a content calendar** that enables you to plan across all channels and platforms.
- **Share the calendar with your entire communications team.** We recommend using Google sheets.
- **Schedule posts in advance** for increased flexibility.
- **Download a free content calendar template** and modify it to incorporate all your communication channels (traditional + digital): SDAdata.blog/calendartemplate.

Schedule Content in Batches

Scheduling your content (and ads) in advance helps you focus on big picture items without the urgency of consistent posting. Plan out regular content in advance and make time to schedule it in monthly or two-week chunks. Then you can focus your attention on engagement, community building, data analysis, strategic planning, and other projects. This also empowers you to be more proactive in your digital strategy, as opposed to reactive—freeing you up to respond quickly to comments or address any unexpected issues or changes.

Budgeting

What's appropriate to spend?

People often ask, "How much does it cost to promote online?" Well, it depends. The beauty of social advertising and other digital promotions is that it the investment is adjustable based on what you can spend. Digital channels (specifically social media) work very well for small budgets and non-profits. A little can go a long way, but it's important to spend at least a little. As your confidence and familiarity with your target audience grows, you can increase your budget gradually. Often, your budget depends on the size of your goals and your purpose. A small local ministry may only need to spend $300 a year to reach the surrounding community, whereas a nationwide campaign would need at least $3,000 to create impact within a targeted audience. Before setting a budget, develop a strategy, strong messaging, and a clear objective. Then start with a small ad budget directed at your target audience. Track and analyze results. Evaluate your results against your ministry's key performance indicators and optimize accordingly. Remember, if you're going to take the time to put together a campaign strategy, take the time to track your performance. Otherwise you can't build on what you've learned or improve for the next campaign, because you didn't learn from the last one. Under the "Distributors" section of this guidebook, we'll discuss advertising in more detail.

Don't Give Up Too Soon!

Post reach and interaction will ebb and flow based on your audience's personal preferences, attitude of the day, the news, that evening's supper, or just the busyness of life. Keep posting. Keep interacting. Keep adapting.

When you initially revamp your digital strategy, the changes in post engagement should show immediate and positive results. But over time things may plateau or even dip, especially during the holidays. You'll learn to see and anticipate yearly patterns. Keep pressing forward. Often efforts fail because people give up too early.

Social Media Best Practices Checklist for Ministries

As previously discussed, a strong digital strategy begins with a good foundation of planning. Social media represents a bold new frontier for mission and is a powerful communications tool. In order to fully realize the untapped potential of the digital mission field, each denominational entity, ministry, or local church is encouraged to download the latest version of the **NAD Social Media Guidelines**[20] for an in-depth manual with *resources and guidance regarding best practices for professional social media communication.*

Whether you're just getting started or conducting a social media audit, this checklist is designed to help you make sure your organization or ministry is maintaining basic best practices for social media.

The Basics

- ☐ **Name:** For all official denominational entities under the North American Division, use the North American Division name alongside your ministry name whenever possible, and include the full division name (not the abbreviation "NAD") in the description for all social media accounts. Please refer to the **NAD Brand Guidelines**[21]. For non-affiliated ministry entities or individuals, be sure to choose a name that accurately reflects your ministry and mission, while staying consistent with your internal guidelines for use.

- ☐ **Consistent branding:** Use the same name, profile image, header images, and bio on each platform to affirm brand recognition and help members identify official accounts.

- ☐ **Logo:** The branding and logo guidelines for the North American Division apply to social media as well as print and all other forms of communication. Please refer to the NAD Brand Guidelines for more information and downloadable logos. For non-affiliated ministry entities or individuals, be sure to develop a consistent logo and internal guidelines for use.

- ☐ **Optimize images per platform:** Be sure to use the optimal image sizes for each social media platform to help your brand stand out and look professional.

- ☐ **Contact information:** Provide additional contact information such as a phone number, business address, and email address, where relevant, in the about section of your social media account profiles.

---

20 "NAD Social Media Guidelines I NAD Digital Evangelism I Columbia, MD." *Digital Evangelism*, www.sdadata.org/social-media-guidelines.html.
21 "Brand Guidelines." Brand Guidelines | *North American Division of Seventh-Day Adventists*, www.nadadventist.org/brand-guidelines.

- ☐ **Ownership:** Posts should appear to come from the official brand of the account, not from individuals. An exception to this rule would be Church or ministry officials providing a public statement.

- ☐ **Organization:** Plan out your regular content and schedule posts in advance whenever possible. We recommend that you create a shared content calendar for your team.

- ☐ **Content:** Post consistently and be sure to always include an image/video, short teaser text, a call-to-action, relevant hashtags, and a link.

- ☐ **Link back to your website:** Your website is your biggest communications tool; link back to your website in most posts.

- ☐ **Promote your social media:** Include your social media handles (names) in all of your other communication channels, such as your website, emails, print material, and spoken announcements.

Account Management

- ☐ **Work Facebook accounts:** We strongly recommend that you create a separate work Facebook account to manage official pages to help separate your work from your personal social media.

- ☐ **Facebook page admins:** Facebook pages should have more than one staff admin on the page to prevent lock-out.

- ☐ **Connected emails:** Never connect an organization's social media profiles to private email addresses or even an individual's work email addresses.

    - ☐ Create a dedicated social media address (socialmedia@yourministry.com) for your organization and grant multiple people access. Contact your IT department for assistance if applicable.

    - ☐ Connect social media accounts like Twitter, Instagram, Snapchat, YouTube, and Hootsuite to the work social media email address.

- ☐ **Page roles and access:** Regularly check Facebook page roles and account access to make sure it is up-to-date and does not include former employees. When social media managers/page editors/admins leave your organization and no longer require access to your social media accounts, update page roles immediately and change passwords to all social media platforms, management accounts, and emails.

Account Protection

- ☐ **Security:** Keep your account privacy and security settings up-to-date with the latest best practices. This also applies to your laptops and devices.

- ☐ **Facebook:** We highly recommend that you set up the following safe-guards:

    - ☐ **Two-factor authentication:** Two-factor authentication creates an extra layer of security when log-ins are attempted from unknown browsers. This will safeguard against hackers who could otherwise take control of personal profiles, organizational pages, ad accounts, and credit cards. .

- [ ] **Trusted contacts:** Choose coworkers to be trusted Facebook contacts to help you regain access to a compromised account.

- [ ] **Follow Facebook's recommended security updates:** Learn more about features and tips at **facebook.com/help**.

- [ ] **Passwords:** For all social media accounts (personal and organizational), please choose strong, unique passwords and change them every six months.

Ideally, organizations should conduct a basic social media audit every six months as part of a larger digital communications strategy review. The digital mission field is dynamic and ever-changing, and the North American Division office of Big Data + Social Media is here to help you stay informed. Once you can check off everything on this list, visit **SDAdata.org** for more resources, tips, and tutorials to continue to enhance your digital evangelism and discipleship strategies.

Branding for Ministries

This process begins with one question

How do you want your organization to be known? This is its brand. Once you understand your organization's mission and purpose (as discussed in the previous section), you can then shape your brand around those goals.

Components of your brand strategy should cover three areas. marketing, public relations, and corporate communication. Think of marketing as evangelism (**OUTREACH**) and corporate communications as internal or member-focused messaging (**INREACH**). Public relations can be understood as what the general community knows, or thinks, about your church or organization. In other words, what are you known for in the community? Too often, our churches are simply "the building on the corner" and not perceived as a center for positive influence.

"Branding is the process of revealing a holistic picture of an organization to its audience by curating a perception, experience, and essence. Brands are communicated, not just created. A brand is based entirely on a person's experience." — Heidi Baumgartner

To help shape this process, ask: What can your church or ministry become known for? What is unique about what your organization has to offer the community?

If you don't already have a ministry name, website domain, and social media handle, choose a name based on your organization's mission or purpose that can be used across all channels. For established ministries, intentionally devising handles and constructing social media profiles can help you reshape or rebrand your image and voice for your online audiences. Base decisions on the vision you want to cast. Determine whether your primary goal falls into either the outreach, inreach, or public relations area. It's possible that your mission may cross over into more than one area. Then brainstorm name/handle ideas with your team, board, or members that could fit into one, two, or all of the three categories below. Through a process of elimination, narrow down the options and come to a final decision. Make sure that, before you identify the top choices, you have first checked their availability on sites like **knowem.com** (social media platforms) and **godaddy.com** (for website domain names).

Ideas for Developing Handles

Refer to the chart on the next page when brainstorming name/handle ideas for your organization.

Your social media handle should reflect your brand and your purpose for being online or using the platform. A handle is a unique identifying username representing your organization. In other words, it's your social media nickname. Keep your handle consistent across all platforms so potential followers can find you easily. It's also a good idea to reserve your handle on a wide range of platforms, even if you aren't able to consistently

PATHS OF CREATIVITY Emphasis: **Marketing** Example: @gorgeous2god	KEYWORD THEME Emphasis: **Public Relations** Example: @enditnowNAD	ORG NAME Emphasis: **Corp. Communication** Example: @NADadventist
• Name concepts that connect to mission and vision • Appeal to external audiences • Promote evangelism (outreach) • Build community within a specific target audience	• Utilize keywords that describe themes/mission • Intentionally blend marketing and corporate communications • Encourage community awareness and influence	• Use the organizational name in various iterations • Focus on internal audiences • Emphasize offical statements, polices, beliefs, etc. • Distribute member information (inreach)

Credit: *Heidi Baumgartner, edited by Jamie Domm*

post on all of them right now, to prevent brand confusion and to save them for future use in case your social media strategy expands. We recommend also choosing a website domain that matches your ministry's name and handle to further reinforce your brand across multiple channels and touchpoints. An example of a ministry with consistent branding is **Gorgeous2God**, whose mission primarily falls under outreach. Their social media handle across all their platforms is **@gorgeous2god**, and their domain is **gorgeous2god.org**. They even utilize a branded hashtag when relevant, **#gorgeous2god**.

Your branding should:

- promote awareness
- foster emotional connectedness
- communicate your mission and values (brand story)
- encourage brand ambassadors
- provide strategic direction to your team and set clear goals/objectives (mission/vision)
- shape expectations for those you serve (brand promise)

Your brand strategy and digital strategy work together and are part of an overarching grand communications strategy that includes, and does not replace, traditional means of outreach and marketing as well as in-person experience.

Redeveloping your brand and your overall communications strategy takes a lot of behind-the-scenes homework. Involve people in your team throughout the process so they could share in ownership and add new insights you may not have considered.

Brand Basics

Brand: represented by its logo, its color, its typefaces, its images, its designs, its tone of voice, and its customer service

Brand strategy: defines the organization's central message and how to say it

Brand guidelines: a system of managing the brand visually

The biggest problem I see with ministries using social media is that they have no clear objectives. You must determine your purpose and shape your online communications and brand accordingly. In addition, determine your target audience, goals and key performance indicators as discussed in the previous section on strong foundations, and conduct a thorough communications and social media audit (examining all touchpoints). Then, based on all your findings, conduct a thorough branding audit, establishing where you currently are and deciding where you want to go. This process helps you to evaluate your overall communication strategies and can direct your rebranding. Once you've defined your purpose(s), shape your brand name, design, and messaging style in a way that will help you steer toward the desired perception and achieve your mission goals.

Next, develop your identity across all platforms and channels as part of your overall brand. Social media does not work in a silo; it should be integrated in your broader communications, both digital and traditional.

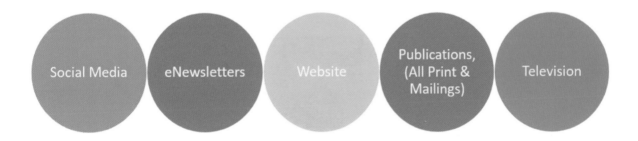

Helpful resource: identity.adventist.org

Establish Branding Consistency

Make sure all your social media profiles look consistent and use the same name.

- Reserve your name on all platforms.
- Use a consistent name (15 characters or less; short/simple; stands test of time; no numbers, symbols, or punctuation).
- Use the same profile photo & a consistent design look.
- Use the same headline, blurb, or bio.

Your digital presence is an extension of your church brand and voice into the online world. Your brand is how your church or ministry is perceived.

- Develop a consistent voice/tone.
- Clearly articulate what you do and offer through your mission, brand promise, and brand story.

How we feel about a brand ultimately stems from our experiences with it. Put yourself in the shoes of a person experiencing your brand for the first time, and view your ministry through an outsider's perspective. Evaluate their experience objectively and make changes based on your communication objectives. Develop a clear **brand promise** (what your organization has to offer) and make sure all aspects of your organization deliver on that promise.

Strong digital brands create connections with real people and take a comprehensive approach to the member experience. **Have guidelines for every part of an audience member's journey**[22] (case study example: Dan Serns, Evangelism Coordinator, Texas Conference of Seventh-day Adventists), including in-person, on-site interactions. Remember every experience—physical or digital—says something about your brand. **Utilize all your possible brand touchpoints (see graphic below) to tell one consistent story**. Remember to view all of your touchpoints as part of a holistic experience, as a seeker does not experience their journey in silos.

Credit: *Heidi Baumgartner, modified by Jamie Domm*

---

22 "Why Not Try This? … Mentor New Members." *Dan Serns*, 29 Jan. 2020, danserns.wordpress.com/2019/08/11/ mentor-new-members/.

How your online followers and community perceive your ministry influences their perception of not only the Church corporately, but God, even if you haven't put any effort into creating or managing your brand. In the absence of your story, people will fill in the blanks themselves. Your digital voice may be the only opportunity your followers have to see Christ's love demonstrated in their life.

People search online for answers to their problems; what better place for the Church to engage them?

But first, we must have a clear understanding of who we are and be able to clearly demonstrate our mission, vision, and value. Create a brand that your target audience can recognize and connect with in a meaningful and positive way.

Having a strong brand and digital communications strategy won't cost a lot of money but will involve a lot of time. Consider this an opportunity to build a team of digital disciples and brand ambassadors within your church or ministry. These people will become the human face and voice of your brand 24/7. Investing in their talent can also positively influence their level of investment in the Church long-term.

Tips for Optimizing
Your Website

Tips for Improving Your Digital Curb Appeal

For the first ten years of my career I had the opportunity to develop my digital skillsets in the secular world with the hope that someday these skills could be used to serve God more directly. I am pleased to say that there is a tide-shift happening now in the Seventh-day Adventist Church at multiple levels; we are collectively waking up to the untapped potential of the digital mission field.

There is potential for a beautiful marriage between traditional means of evangelism and digital communications. These new technologies are not meant to entirely replace the old methods, but serve to magnify and increase the scale of our efforts in a way that was not thought possible a few decades ago.

*First Impressions
Matter to Seekers*

I spend a lot of time with seasoned evangelists who share wisdom from their experiences in the physical mission field. Many of their proven principles for effective evangelism have direct application in the digital space. To truly move forward with our mission, mentorship and education must go in two directions. Not only can the younger generations teach the older generation about technology and demonstrate how it can be used to advance our cause, but the younger, digitally-focused generations can learn much from the giants of traditional evangelism. Instead of getting frustrated by our different perspectives, we must communicate more effectively with each other to understand our common ground. Like a giant ship set in its regular route, it takes time to turn, and it takes all crew members working together.

The methods by which we minister to people and share the gospel are becoming more complex, but human nature, needs, and behavior largely stays the same and are predictable. One "analog" idea that can be translated to the digital space is the idea of "curb appeal." Long before the internet and 360° video, real-estate agents focused their attention on finding ways to optimize something called "curb appeal" (aka the outward appearance of a property). If someone was interested in buying a house, they most likely would drive by it before calling the agent to request a walk-through. For churches, the behavior of prospective visitors was similar. Pastors and ministry leaders sought to make the outside of their church inviting for potential visitors. This is still important today, but now we have the added need for "digital curb appeal."

The following statistics indicate why

- 97% of people search for local organizations online (**Adaptive Marketing**[23]).

- 76% of mobile shoppers have changed their mind about which retailer or brand to buy from after searching on Google (**Google Data**[24]).

- Nearly half (46%) of people say a website's design is their number one criterion for determining the credibility of an organization (**Hubspot**[25]).

- 46% of church attendees said that a church's website was important in picking a church to visit (**Network.crcna.org**[26]).

- 33% of people said that the internet was initially where they learned about their church (**Network.crcna.org**[27]).

- In 2015, Facebook influenced 52% of consumers' online and offline purchases, up from 36% in 2014 (**The Drum**[28]).

It's clear that an organization's digital presence affects behavior. What do people find when they Google your ministry or find you on social media platforms? Is the content up-to-date? Is new visitor information easy to find? Are there pictures, testimonies, and stories that reflect your church community and appear inviting to others? Is it clear what services and opportunities your church, ministry, or organization provides?

According to a **LifeWay Research**[29] survey, "78% of churches have a website, [but] only 30-40% of churches are using their websites for anything other than an electronic bulletin board! And about 42% hardly keep their websites up to date?!" (**Churchleaders.com**[30]) The same is true with social media. Are you posting regularly and is all the essential information current? For many, your digital presence will be their first introduction to your ministry and possibly, the faith as a whole. Many people will find your website long before they physically visit a place of worship. A study by **Grey Matter Research**[31] found that, in the span of one year, "over 17 million American adults who don't regular attend worship services visited the website of a local church or place of worship."

---

23 Kolowich, Lindsay. "16 Stats That Prove the Importance of Local SEO." *HubSpot Blog*, blog.hubspot.com/marketing/local-seo-stats.

24 "A Marketer's Guide to Holiday Supershoppers." *Google*, Google, www.thinkwithgoogle.com/advertising-channels/mobile-marketing/marketing-guide-holiday-shopping-2016/.

25 Sibley, Amanda. "19 Reasons You Should Include Visual Content in Your Marketing [Data]." *HubSpot Blog*, blog.hubspot.com/blog/tabid/6307/bid/33423/19-Reasons-You-Should-Include-Visual-Content-in-Your-Marketing-Data.aspx.

26 Clark, Jerod, and Jerod Clark. "Church Website Statistics." *The Network*, network.crcna.org/church-web/church-website-statistics.

27 Clark, Jerod, and Jerod Clark. "Church Website Statistics." *The Network*, network.crcna.org/church-web/church-website-statistics.

28 McCarthy, John. "Facebook Influences over Half of Shoppers Says DigitasLBi's Connected Commerce Report." *The Drum*, The Drum, 20 Aug. 2015, www.thedrum.com/news/2015/04/24/facebook-influences-over-half-shoppers-says-digitaslbi-s-connected-commerce-report.

29 "LifeWay Research." *LifeWay Research*, lifewayresearch.com/.

30 Starner, Matthew, et al. "Churches & Websites: Come on! You Can Do Better!" *ChurchLeaders*, 14 June 2012, churchleaders.com/worship/worship-how-tos/161409-churches-websites-come-on-you-can-do-better.html.

31 Huss, Richard, and Steven Gliebe. "Getting Church Website Visitors Through Your Doors." *ChurchThemes.com*, 5 Oct. 2018, churchthemes.com/church-website-visitors-through-doors/.

Your ministry's website and social media are your biggest digital marketing and branding tools, and it's where first impressions are made. If your congregation members engage with the corporate Church accounts on social media, it's likely others are seeing their interactions and could be discouraged OR encouraged to visit your local church based on the kind of content posted. Tell your local story through your website and social media. Reveal a community that others want to join. Your website is a means of communicating, in general terms, everything that your church or ministry offers to a prospective visitor. It's your "curb appeal." Your social media can further demonstrate the type of community they will experience and what sort of spiritual messages they will receive.

Importance of Mobile

When people search for local businesses using a smartphone, 76% of them visit a related location within one day (**Think with Google**[32]). As of August 2019, BrightEdge reported 62% of a large sample group conducted their search queries on mobile devices, including tablets, as opposed to computers.

Making your website mobile friendly is more vital than ever, especially since Google prioritizes mobile-friendly content in the search algorithm.

I recommend that you regularly conduct an audit of your website and social media to:

Your website design is up to date and mobile-friendly. You don't need technical skills or a lot of money to have a professional, high-quality website. Aim for a simplistic look that shows an organized and logical layout. An advantage of drag-and-drop platforms like **Wordpress** or **Wix.com** is that they offer ongoing software and design updates as well as easy-to-edit responsive (mobile-friendly) templates—all for an annual hosting fee as low as $100. If you have a staff member with more technical expertise and want to be **NAD branding compliant**[33], the website branding pattern system ALPS is set up to be installed in a WordPress site.

Make sure essential information is accurate, up to date, and easy to find. Remember, empathy first. Put yourself in a prospective visitor's place and seek to understand their needs and/or experience. Location, directions, and worship times should be visible on your homepage. Have a "Plan Your Visit" section with "What to Expect" FAQs. Not knowing what to expect is a barrier to entry for many people. This information can be included on both your website and Facebook. Links to this information can be listed on other social media platforms.

Tell your story in the "About" section and share what you believe. Do your images on the website and social media reflect your congregation and culture? Do your listed core values and beliefs match what they will experience in person? To really connect

32 "A Marketer's Guide to Holiday Supershoppers." *Google*, Google, www.thinkwithgoogle.com/advertising-channels/mobile-marketing/marketing-guide-holiday-shopping-2016/.
33 "Adventist Identity Guidelines | NAD Digital Evangelism | Columbia, MD." *Digital Evangelism*, www.sdadata.org/adventist-identity-guidelines.html.

with people, we must relate to their core values and needs. Write in a conversational and friendly tone to make your audience feel informed and valued. Make sure you communicate clearly to prospective visitors, and most importantly, reflect the love of Christ always. Much of this content can be "evergreen" with little need for regular updates.

Showcase opportunities. Are all your upcoming events, ministry projects, and youth activities listed? If you don't have the staffing for regular updates, present your opportunities in general terms and ask them to join your email list and/or like your Facebook page for event notices. Generally, church members do not check their own website, so shape your content around the needs of a visitor. Again, if you don't have the resources for weekly website updates, present material that is "evergreen," contact information on how a potential visitor can learn more. Once they step in the door, be sure to have a **welcoming strategy**[34] to help them build relationships and get plugged into church life.

Strong brands create connection and take a comprehensive approach to the member experience. Today, that experience often begins online. Your digital presence should make them want to experience your faith/mission in person, motivating them towards action.

---

34 "Why Not Try This? ... Mentor New Members." Dan Serns, 29 Jan. 2020, danserns.wordpress.com/2019/08/11/mentor-new-members/.

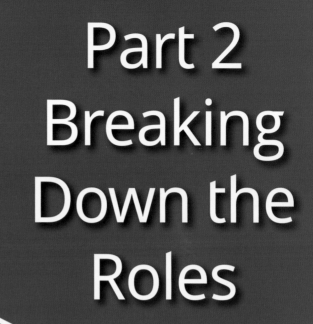

Part 2
Breaking Down the Roles

Creatives

searching

keyword ...

What Role Do Content Creators (Creatives) Play?

People search online for answers to their problems. What better place for the Church to share its message of hope and wholeness?

Our message is the gospel. It's the role of creatives to package it in ways that connect with our audiences by using the platforms, tools, language, and media that are culturally relevant and accessible to them. Today, that means presenting the gospel message and teachings of Jesus via various digital friendly formats such as video, blogs, images, podcasts, etc. Remember, good communication is when you communicate in a way your audience understands. That requires adaption, whether it's the physical mission field or the digital one.

Content As Mission: Think Differently

Before we get into the practical application of content creation, I want to challenge the status quo for a moment. Only **20% of Americans regularly attend church**[35], and only **2 in 10 millennials consider regular church attendance important**[36]. What if your digital content is the only exposure to the gospel a person receives? How important it is, then, to post consistently! The predominant way the Church uses digital communications currently is to promote events. Promoting events is okay, and we should continue doing that as part of a comprehensive communication strategy. However, we can and should go beyond promoting events to create content that is meaningful and relevant to people's daily lives and challenges. After all, our message is *the gospel*, not "Come to our next event!"

The truth is, some people may never come to church, but we can still touch their lives. How would you witness if your local church service, events, and Bible studies did not exist? What would you want your community to know about Jesus? We're called to preach the gospel, especially to those outside the church body. What ways can you accomplish that? Strategize, find solutions, and fulfill them intentionally.

Put Jesus/God on Display

The life, character, and gift of Jesus Christ should be on display in your digital content and interactions. Jesus came not to uplift Himself, but to reveal an accurate picture of God's character. It's not about how many followers you have on your digital platforms, but how people can and do discover Jesus through you. It's about portraying the truth of God's character in all aspects of our lives, including in the digital space.

---

35 Outreach Magazine. "7 Startling Facts: An Up Close Look at Church Attendance in America." *ChurchLeaders*, 19 July 2019, churchleaders.com/pastors/pastor-articles/139575-7-startling-facts-an-up-close-look-at-church-attendance-in-america.html.
36 "Study Analysis: 6 Reasons Why Only 2 in 10 Millennials Believe Church Attendance Is Important." *The Christian Post*, www.christianpost.com/news/study-analysis-6-reasons-why-only-two-in-10-millennials-believe-church-attendance-is-important-116882/.

We've been going about digital missions backwards. We're spending most of our time and energy promoting events, resources, or products, when we should be ministering first to the needs of our community, just like Jesus demonstrated.

During His three-and-a-half-year ministry, Jesus:

- shared stories
- shared Godly (and scripture-based) wisdom
- attended to people's needs, physically and spiritually
- answered people's questions regarding spiritual matters and everyday challenges
- gave them hope
- created community
- developed an engaged/active church body
- lead people to wholeness
- equipped people to be disciples and to replicate the model He developed

We can use social media and digital tools to achieve our mission of spreading the gospel and helping people by creating content that focuses on mental, physical, and spiritual needs first. Once this foundation is established, we can invite our audience to "taste and see that the Lord is good" (Psalm 34:8, NIV). When used for digital discipleship and evangelism, this shift in focus is a way we can follow Jesus' example for everyday ministry to real people. We can use social influence for kingdom building while utilizing modern tools and technologies.

Christianity is a Lifestyle

Creatives can use their talents online to encourage Christian lifestyles in their community. When asked:

> *"Which commandment is the most important of all?" Jesus answered, "The most important is, 'Hear, O Israel: The Lord our God, the Lord is one. And you shall love the Lord your God with all your heart and with all your soul and with all your mind and with all your strength.' The second is this: 'You shall love your neighbor as yourself.' There is no other commandment greater than these" (Mark 12:28-31, ESV).*

True Christianity is about helping those in need and seeking ways to elevate the well-being of others, all while reflecting the character of Christ. One way to do that is to create sharable content. But what is shareable content? In other words, what kind of online content do people tend to interact with and share with their friends? What makes content relevant or worthy of sharing?

Hootsuite reported on an extensive study[37] conducted by the New York Times to uncover the top reasons people share content online.

The top five reasons why people share online are:

- "To improve the lives of others" (94%)
- "To get the word out about causes they believe in" (84%)
- "To grow and nourish relationships" (80%)
- "To define themselves" (68%)
- "Self-fulfillment"

The number one reason people share content is that they feel it will improve the lives of their followers/friends. Amazingly, this is a core Christian value and could be developed in coordination with digital media for the gospel message. As digital evangelists and disciples, it's an essential part of our mission to share and create content that will uplift, help, and/or improve the lives of your audience (and their audiences). Eighty-four percent of participants in the NYT study also said that they share information "because it is a way to support causes or issues they care about" (**New York Times**[38]), which directly relates to the first reason. Think about how your mission **aligns with the core values of your target audience**[39] and create content that supports these values. In fact, the Church should be the clear leader in using its digital influence to create media content that improves the lives of others and advocates for meaningful causes.

Sharing content online is also a means by which many maintain and create relationships. This is an incentive for us to create content that helps foster connections between members of our community, our brand, and Christ. Encourage engagement and conversation as much as possible. Additionally, people use their social influence to help create an "idealized online persona" of themselves. Evaluate your audience's interests and develop content that fits with their goals or identity. Ask: "How can our organization's content demonstrate what it means to be a follower of Christ?" or, "How can our ministry's content create value for those already invested in supporting our mission and interested in becoming more involved in our community?"

Finally, the same research found that "consumers enjoy content more when they share it, and that they enjoy content more when it is shared with them." When we create audience-focused content that facilitates this sense of positive community and interactions, we can help encourage our audience's natural desire to share our content for perceived personal and social value.

The Seventh-day Adventist Church has a solid message that can easily meet the top motivations for sharing content online, but presentation is everything. It's up to content

---

37 "Social Media and Psychology: 8 Lessons for Marketers." *Hootsuite Social Media Management*, 2 May 2019, blog.hootsuite.com/social-media-psychology/.

38 https://www.bostonwebdesigners.net/wp-content/uploads/POS_PUBLIC0819-1.pdf

39 "Understanding Your Target Audience for Effective Communication." *Digital Evangelism*, www.sdadata.org/digital-evangelism-blog/understanding-your-target-audience-for-effective-communication.

creators to package our messages so that they clearly align with the type of content people want to share. The tools and technologies will continue to change, but people and their deepest desires and motivations generally remain the same.

Empathy: Think Like a Seeker

Always remember: empathy first. Put yourself in a prospective visitor/viewer/engager's place and seek to understand their needs and/or experience. Figure out what their barriers to entry or barriers to faith are, and try to diminish or address them through the content you create, services you provide, and the relationships you build. Create an online space for community, love, support, and understanding through your content.

When creating, consider who might engage with your media.

"These five key motivations clearly show that your audience's main reasons for sharing are their relationships with other people—not your brand. Keep this in mind as you continue creating and sharing audience-focused content." — Dara Fontein, Hootsuite

Ask yourself:

- What questions might my audience have that I can answer?
- What questions could they have about my church or beliefs?
- What questions might they have about God?
- What would encourage them to attend a church or reach out to a Christian to better understand Jesus, salvation, or the Bible?
- What issues are they facing?
- What could encourage or help them in hard times?
- What are their barriers to faith or barriers to entry in my church?

Our goal as content creators is to reveal who God really is in a world that often views God, or religion in general, as vindictive, cruel, and uncaring.

Don't just create content for content's sake. Consider:

"How will your audience change as a result of your [article/letter/post/video]?"
—Seth Godin, marketing guru

Or, more directly applicable to our mission, ask:

How will their attitude and perceptions of God change because of your [article/letter/post/video]?

Basics of Content Creation and Strategy

Before we get started, we must first answer the question, "Who is a content creator?" The ultimate source of creative content and inspiration will always be the Bible and God. Therefore, those of us who answer the call to share the gospel online must always look first to Jesus Christ and His word for guidance.

Social media is the ultimate equalizer. It gives a voice and a platform to anyone willing to engage. —Amy Jo Martin

Social media and modern technologies have eased entry into the world of telling stories, sharing ideas, and expressing thoughts through creative visual content to a wide audience. We can all be writers, creatives, and publishers now. This means that when it comes to creating content for evangelism and discipleship, the role is no longer restricted to pastors, theologians, and other trained professionals. Church leaders can organize teams of content creators within their churches and ministries by empowering professionals or aspiring young people with expertise in design, video, communications, writing, technology, etc. Many congregations have yet to tap into the potential of tech savvy members and their modern-day spiritual gifts. Greater collaboration across multiple generations can be fostered by investing in young people and giving them space to utilize their skills in this area for the Church.

Organize Your Team

There's no single way to organize your team(s), given that every ministry is unique. Start by taking an inventory of your church's human resources and individuals' personal interests and skills. Then organize accordingly to best accomplish your goals and utilize your church body's strengths and talents. Determine roles and responsibilities, set up a multi-channel content calendar that can be shared with everyone on the team, and map out your content strategy, being sure to take an integrative approach that incorporates both traditional and digital methods of communication.

Download a content calendar template[40] (be sure to customize it to reflect your channels). We recommend using Google Docs for sharing the content planning calendar with your team.

Remember the "Rule of 7"

If you recall from the "Strong Foundations[41]" section, the "Rule of 7" states that a person needs to be exposed to a message at least seven times before they'll take a desired action. Develop a comprehensive content strategy that incorporates both traditional media and digital, working together to maximize impact. In most cases, digital media is not used in place of traditional forms of communication, but in addition, as a means of amplifying your message to a larger community. Implementing an effective content strategy requires repeated, consistent messaging from multiple communication channels. Plan to repackage your content for different platforms and channels. If we view evangelism holistically, every touchpoint matters, as your target audience is likely to come in contact with several.

These touchpoints may include, but are not limited to:

Traditional: printed outreach materials, presentations, events, classes, seminars, wearables/flare, ephemera, print/radio advertising, direct mail pieces, billboards, flyers, bulletins, print newsletters, print publications/literature, other handouts, signage, posters, branded vehicles, letterhead, business cards, general resources, radio ministry

Digital: digital advertising messages and design, digital newsletters/emails, digital publications/blogs, digital flyers, website(s), social media content, videos, online resources, podcasts

With this in mind, try utilizing a diversity of content, touchpoints, and channels that are relevant to your mission to help reinforce the same "story" or message in unique ways to maximize effectiveness.

The 20/80 Rule

Whether you realize it or not, your communications and content (or lack thereof) are telling a story, and that story is key to giving your audience a sense of why your ministry is valuable. When your audience values what you're doing, they are more likely to respond to your call-to-actions and actively participate in other ways.

Social media is popular because it speaks to a basic human need: to connect and share. We must use digital media to tell our "story" all day, every day, and build a connection with our community that ultimately motivates them to draw closer to Christ.

Along with the "Rule of 7," you'll want to incorporate the 20/80 principle in your content planning. The ideal ratio of posts on an organization's digital media should be 20% direct appeals (calls-to-action to get involved, donate, register, etc.), 80% engagement. In other words, 80% of the content posted by your ministry should:

- demonstrate the need your organization fulfills through services it provides,

---

41 "It All Begins with a Strong Foundation." *Digital Evangelism*, www.sdadata.org/digital-evangelism-blog/it-all-begins-with-a-strong-foundation.

- share what initiatives your ministry is implementing to satisfy the felt needs of your community,
- update your audience on your various goals and efforts,
- showcase impact through testimonials and results,
- and engage and connect with your followers.

Think of social media as a potluck with friends during which you share your desire to go on a mission trip, or your excitement about an upcoming event you're organizing. You wouldn't hard sell them or ask them for their involvement with no context, but you might talk about your goals, ambitions, why it's important, and why you're excited about what you have planned. Once your friends understand how important this mission trip or event is, they will naturally be more inclined to help you when you mention that you haven't yet reached your fundraising goal, or they may even accept your invitation to attend with you.

The same principle is true for an organization's social media channels. If you spend most of your efforts telling the story behind your ministry and creating value, your followers will gradually become more emotionally invested. Then, when you make direct appeals for action (the 20%), you will have better results because your supporters feel like they understand the importance of your mission, know what to expect, and know how the money will be used. This is especially important for millennial givers, who demand transparency and accountability when it comes to use of funds.

Plan Efficiently

Social media can seem daunting, but it doesn't have to be. For most Adventist entities, social media manager is just one of many hats an employee or volunteer might wear. If you happen to be a full-time digital strategist, you're likely managing multiple campaigns and projects at once. Regardless of your level of expertise, there never seems to be enough time in the day to accomplish everything you need to do in order to stay on top of the ever-growing evangelistic influence of digital media. Streamlining your approach will help you and your team tackle a large workload.

Here are our top three tried-and-true time-saving tips for developing your content and/or campaign strategy:

1. **Schedule your content in batches.** Scheduling your content (and ads) in advance helps you focus on big picture items without the urgency of consistent posting. Plan out regular content in advance and make time to schedule it in monthly or bi-weekly chunks. Then you can focus your attention on engagement, community building, data analysis, strategic planning, and other projects. Staying on top of performance analytics enables you to better evaluate and optimize your strategy, ultimately helping you reach your campaign goals. This technique empowers you to be more proactive in your digital strategy, as opposed to reactive. You'll also have more flexibility to respond quickly to comments or address any unexpected issues or changes.

2. **Create evergreen content and repurpose posts.** Just because you posted a piece of content once doesn't mean your entire audience has seen it or had the time to react. Remember the "Rule of 7" states that a person must see a message at least seven times before they take action. Consequently, it's a good idea to use one post multiple times to ensure greater exposure. Over the course of several months, you can schedule pieces of evergreen content with slightly different wording and images, and post at different times of day and different days of the week to reach different groups of people. Evergreen content is content that maintains it's relevancy indefinitely, without losing its usefulness after a certain time period.

   This enables your team to invest more time into creating compelling posts and strong resources, videos, and images that could be used multiple times, instead of constantly seeking to create new original content. Then, weave new content around these evergreen posts as it becomes available. This technique helps guarantee a consistent posting schedule and continuous flow of content.

   For event-specific campaigns, you can leverage the technique of repurposing to build urgency towards deadlines. For example, as the last day for an early-bird registration approaches, you can rework the same message and call-to-action using key buzzwords to attract attention.

   Messaging example:

   - 2 weeks until the early-bird discount ends!

   - Early-bird registration ends THIS Friday. Register today!

   - Don't miss out! The discount price for registration ends tomorrow. Sign up now!

   Then utilize the scheduling in advance technique and set up the posts ahead of time, as well as any targeted social ads you have planned.

3. **Build off previous campaign plans for reoccurring events.** This is possibly our biggest hack for annual or repeating conferences and programs. Always keep your strategy outline and performance report from the previous campaign. For the next project, simply reuse what worked, change what didn't, update/tweak the content and timing for the new event, and freshen up the images. Systematically building off the previous campaign improves campaign performance and results each time you make adjustments that strengthen it. By tracking each campaign performance and studying the results, you not only continue to reach your audience more effectively, but lower overall costs. Why reinvent the wheel, when you can just improve it?

Repurpose What You Already Produce

No need to start from scratch; your team is probably already doing a good job generating content related to newsworthy events or outreach. Packaging it for the digital space and publishing online enables you to grow your potential audience exponentially beyond the worship service. A great amount of what your team may already produce for your local church ministries is content, for example: sermons and live-streams each week, studies for small groups, messages from the pastor in newsletters, videos, pictures from events, testimonials, etc. Always look for content you are already creating, then consider how it can be repackaged and weaved into your overall digital content strategy. This can be inexpensive and have long-term value as the content stays in place and is relevant for people to discover far into the future. Prioritize content that will help your audience in a tangible way, either emotionally, physically, spiritually, or psychologically.

Finding Relevant Content Ideas For Your Target Audience

If you're like many content creators, you've hit a creative roadblock at some point. It doesn't matter if you're a pastor, Christian vlogger, or a digital disciple; we have all run out of content ideas and sat staring at our laptops at some point. As digital evangelists, we want to create relevant content, but may not always be sure what people are searching for online. Our purpose is to meet the needs of people in the digital space, and luckily, the inspiration we need lies in tools many of us use every day. Being strategic and intentional with the content we create, can help us provide people with the answers and connection they are searching for.

I've said this before: **people are literally Googling for God**, and I don't expect this to change anytime soon.

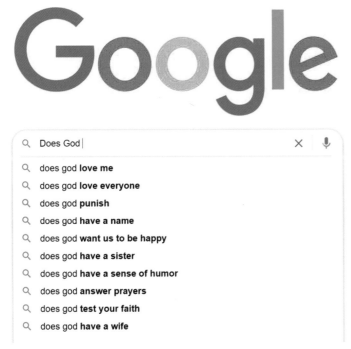

Each year there are millions of Google searches for answers to questions like:

- Is God real?
- What happens when we die?
- How do I know I'm saved?
- Why is there so much suffering in the world?

There is a great need for our message of hope and wholeness. Additionally, many people are hurting emotionally, entertaining suicidal thoughts, or feel there is no hope for their situation. They turn to the internet for companionship, understanding, information, anonymity, and more. It's easier for them to pour out their heartfelt searching to Google or on social media than it is to talk to a friend, neighbor, co-worker, or family member. Consequently, this is where we, as disciples, need to cast our net. We need to provide the kind of spiritual food the fish are looking to feed on.

Here is an easy tip for a wealth of content ideas

Find content, write content, and curate content related to top Google searches. Frame your posts to pique curiosity and answer people's questions, addressing their deepest longings. You can get top search data from any search engine, YouTube, and other social media trend tracking sites. Try it. Start typing in a question and let the search engine auto-finish. The top results represent the most popular search queries. In other words, you will see what large numbers of people are searching for online. It gives you a sneak peek into their needs, worries, nagging questions, and often hidden yearnings.

These trends allow us to predict what topics audiences may find interesting, and we can use this predictability to speak to the masses in a relevant way. When we make content that speaks to people's spiritual needs and seeks to address their deepest longings, we can change lives through digital evangelism. Being strategic and intentional with the content we create allows us to provide people with the answers and connection they are looking for online.

Bonus Tips

1. Explore **Google Trends**[42] for more ideas that can be specific to your location.
2. Name your blog post, video, etc. the same as the search result you're basing your content on, so the search engines match it to that specific query. This helps your content appear higher in the search results and receive greater visibility. For

example, you could start typing "Does God..." into the Google search box and choose the top-ranking query in the example above: "...test us." Then create a blog post and/or video named "Does God test us?"

Jesus Spent Time with People

"You must come close to those for whom you labor, that they may not only hear your voice, but shake your hand, learn your principles, feel your sympathy."
—*Ellen White, Ministry of Healing*

I cannot stress this enough: *while data and research can be a huge asset when trying to find relevant content to create and issues to address, nothing replaces quality time with those you are seeking to reach. The best thing you can do in order to understand the needs and interests[43] of your audience is to engage with them in person. Talk to them, ask questions, show them you care, and dig deep into their perspectives and challenges. This kind of relationship-building can also take place in the digital space when necessary.*

Additional Content Tips & Ideas

- Try new things and see how your audience responds.
- Crowd-source content from your church community (members' content as well as conference, union, and division resources) to help when you have limited time or manpower. You don't have to create everything.
- Break the scroll, think differently, and allow creativity in your team.
- Build predictability/expectations for when new content will be released (like a new blog post every week or new podcast episode released on the first of each month) but don't be so predictable it's boring.
- Develop a multi-generational creative team with room to innovate and fail.
- Lower the barrier to entry by demonstrating what it's like to be a part of your church community. Peel back the corporate-ness of a brand to reveal humanity by featuring behind the scenes videos and live streams.
- Put your church culture on display. Give your audience a glimpse of the events, spiritual life, and friends they might make.
- Champion your ministries, team, and member achievements online.
- Find ways to showcase how non-members could fit in and be welcomed in your church.
- Tell stories, and share experiences and testimonies online.
- Offer digital bible studies, live-streamed prayer sessions, webinars, etc.
- Share inspirational passages, health nuggets, practical advice for day-to-day challenges, marriage and parenting tips, community alerts, resources relevant to community issues, etc.

Content Tips for Personal Digital Discipleship

Start slow, if sharing spiritual content online is new to you and your friends. However, continue to be your authentic, unique self, who is also in a public relationship with Jesus. Share your interests but find natural ways to weave in your faith. Over time, it will get easier.

Share practical content that is relevant to you and helps "prepare the soil" for future conversations with people within your sphere of influence.

Some examples, as described by Communications Executive Rachel Lemons Aitken, could include:

- o Relationship articles
- o Lifestyle content
- o Healthy living headlines
- o Videos showing healthy food being prepared
- o Recipes
- o Workout tips
- o How you're making health changes in your life
- o Mental and emotional health tips

The Purpose of Content

Digital media grants the community the immediate ability to sense what your church is about by seeing its:

- Content
- Personalities
- Culture
- Environments
- Beliefs
- Services to the community

However, in order for your digital content to be effective, your online visitors must actually feel welcomed to attend in person, transforming online engagements and conversations into an on-site, in-person experience. Remember those brand touchpoints discussed earlier. A person's perception of your church and faith will be based almost entirely on experiences they've had interacting with your organization (brand).

Your digital strategy must go beyond "content out, bodies in." Strive to create content that moves people through their spiritual journey. Find ways to feed your community's spiritual needs beyond the few hours they spend in a church service each week. Provide spiritual guidance to those people who may never come to a church service. Afterall, the kingdom of God is an all-day, every-day pursuit. His Church and teachings should be available 24/7.

Done is Better Than Perfect

People are drawn to authenticity in communications, not perfection. This trend is likely to hold true over the next decade, and this is good news for content creators. There is a place for highly produced professional content, but don't let resource or skill-set limitations prevent you from attempting to create valuable content.

Remember

God doesn't call the qualified, He qualifies the called.

Keep learning and keep trying. You and your team will improve with time and practice. Your videos and content do not always have to be produced pieces, nor should they be, in order to optimize relatability and impact. In fact, overly produced content can turn people away. That doesn't mean be sloppy or allow for typos, but understand that you're not competing with Fortune 500 advertising campaigns or mega-church branding. Local churches and ministries have the advantage when it comes to showcasing real people, authenticity, and community in a way that doesn't feel contrived. Don't hesitate to go live on your mission trip, post your event pictures, and share your in-the-moment thoughts online.

Fail Productively

It's fine to fail, just make sure you learn. Not every idea will be a winner, but each piece of content you produce enables you and your team to see in real-time what resonates with people and what doesn't. Your team, through trial and error, can steer toward content that is most impactful to your target audience. Digital media allows us to test, change, and update our content and messages until we get it right, without the burden of high costs. Remember, you're not in this alone. The Holy Spirit is working alongside you. Your message might only reach a limited number of eyes at first, but it could be the exact message those people needed to hear. Small impact doesn't necessarily mean no impact.

A Deeper Dive into Content & Creative Planning Through Keyword Research

People value content that helps them make better decisions, answers their questions, and speaks to their core values or interests. Optimizing your content based on search engine queries (what people are searching for) helps you best match your products and resources to the needs and interests of your audience. We previously took a bird's-eye look at using search results to find relevant content ideas. This section will go into greater depth for those ministries who want to focus more on creating digital content related to their mission and themes. If you're a digital missionary looking to develop a content creation strategy that will reach beyond a geographical location, bookmark this section. This type of digital evangelism helps expand your messaging to new audiences who are hungry for the resources you can provide.

Writer's block? Find out what people are searching for

Keyword[44] **research** is the core of what is known as SEO copywriting: writing content based on search engine optimization principles. Search engine optimization is a set of strategies that help organizations reach more of their online target audience. A website's visibility in search engine results can be elevated by utilizing certain content development techniques. The higher a website ranks when a person googles search terms related to it, the more web traffic it receives. Visit **SDAdata.org/SEO** to learn more about SEO.

Researching keywords removes much of the guesswork when trying to figure out which topics (related to your ministry and mission) make the most sense to explore for your content. It bridges the gap between your hunches, the data, and what information people need or want.

This technique uses search query data from Google and other search engines to determine what kind of topics interest people. Creating content focused on commonly searched topics improves the visibility of your content in search results, which helps users find your ministry and increases the impact of your message.

Use the following framework as a guide to creating content based on keywords.

1) Define the main topic of your online ministry.

For example, you decide you want to start a blog to help Pathfinder leaders.

"Pathfinders," of course, is the topic. But if you title your blog, "Pathfinders," it's not specific enough to get search traffic. You have to differentiate from Nissan Pathfinders, Pathfinder International, and the Pathfinder role-playing game.

---

44 "Keyword Research: The Beginner's Guide to SEO." *Moz*, moz.com/beginners-guide-to-seo/keyword-research.

Familiarity with your audience allows you to feature relevant keywords in your titles, headlines, and posts, such as:

- Pathfinder leadership
- Pathfinder club meetings
- Pathfinder honors
- Pathfinder investiture
- Pathfinder campouts

While definitely more specific than "Pathfinder" alone, these are also considered **broad-match keywords**, as they can still have a wide variety of subtopics. They're certainly good ideas, and posts on these topics can be helpful for your audience. However, they're harder to rank for in Google search results without further specificity.

Let's say there is a burgeoning trend to create Pathfinder blogs. The broad topic of Pathfinder leadership is now a highly competitive arena. How do you get your blog to stand out? Considering the clear, central purpose of your ministry is a useful exercise for most types of digital content, but you'll quickly need to distinguish how you'll be providing something different from the competition.

2) Refine your topic.

You have to get more specialized in your focus, so start brainstorming "**niche topics**"—subtopics within the broad subjects of Pathfinders and meetings and honors and campouts that people might be searching for information about. Some of these might be:

- Pathfinder knot-tying honor
- Pathfinder winter campouts
- Pathfinder club meeting activities
- Pathfinder Bible Experience prep
- Pathfinder Oshkosh fundraising ideas

These are considered **long-tail keywords**[45], or keyphrases. Long-tail keywords are low volume and highly-focused search queries that tend to convert visitors to engaged readers/followers exceptionally well.

You can also start brainstorming possible blog, social media, and video posts for these subtopics and long-tail keywords:

- How to teach knot-tying to Pathfinders
- Make your Pathfinder Investiture fun and memorable
- Top 10 activities for Pathfinder campouts

---

45 Hallebeek, Willemien, et al. "What Are Long-Tail Keywords? • Yoast." *Yoast*, 2 Jan. 2020, yoast.com/what-are-long-tail-keywords/.

- Tips for teaching Pathfinders with disabilities
- Preparing your Pathfinders for Pathfinder Bible Experience
- Best Pathfinder fundraising ideas to cover Oshkosh expenses

3) Test your topic.

Start by googling your topics, exploring related words or phrases, and come up with some post ideas. Then ask yourself the following questions:

- What exists already?
- Can you improve on what's already written?
- Are there certain aspects of the topic that aren't already covered in depth (or at all)?
- How are other users responding to this competing content? Review their comments on posts.

This is your first peek at your opportunities to enter the discussion.

Maybe you find that the knot-tying honor already has several articles that are well-written and popular. There are lots of positive comments on those posts. Therefore, another topic would be more effective in making your content stand out in search results.

However, maybe there's one particular knot you don't feel the other writers have explained very well, even though the rest of the post is good. Maybe you've found a couple comments on other blogs about how they'd like more information on the hunter's bend. You might then decide to write a post titled "How to teach the hunter's bend knot."

This is a simple example of how research and testing can help shape meaningful content creation.

4) Test some more.

Here's where dedicated keyword research tools come in.

These tools access data that tells how many people are searching for a certain keyword or keyphrase (search volume), as well as how much content already exists about that keyword (competition). The sweet spot is when you find a word or phrase that has high search volume and low competition.

Here's an example from **Google Keyword Planner**[46]:

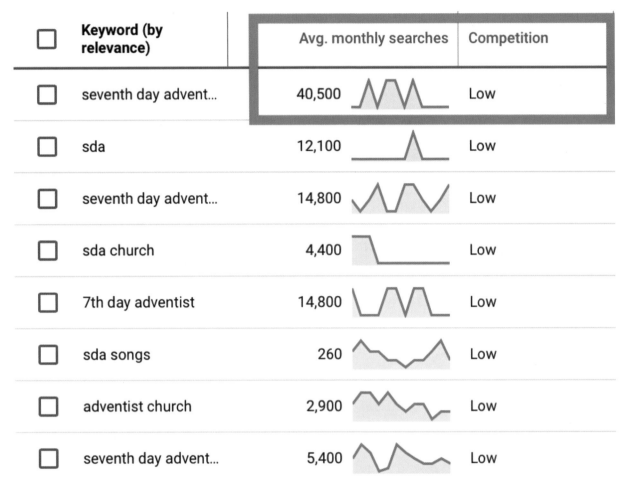

Keyword (by relevance)	Avg. monthly searches		Competition
seventh day advent...	40,500		Low
sda	12,100		Low
seventh day advent...	14,800		Low
sda church	4,400		Low
7th day adventist	14,800		Low
sda songs	260		Low
adventist church	2,900		Low
seventh day advent...	5,400		Low

Many keyword research tools provide a ratio of search volume and competition. Some tools do require a paid subscription, but some are completely free and offer similar data. These free keyword tools may also show related keywords or phrases, which can be helpful for coming up with good content ideas. Overall, you'll get a general idea of what people are searching for, enabling you to create content that will connect your ministry with the needs and interests of your audience.

Here are some recommended free or low-cost tools for keyword research or keyword ideas:

Keywords Everywhere[47] is a browser add-on for Chrome and Firefox that gathers data on every term you search for with Google. It's especially easy to use since you don't have to open a separate program; it already displays keyword results on the side of your browser window. It can also help you find related topics to cover in support of your main topic.

---

46 "Choose the Right Keywords with Our Research Tools." Google Ads, *Google,* ads.google.com/home/tools/keyword-planner/.
47 "Browser Add-on to See Google Search Volume Everywhere." *Keywords Everywhere,* keywordseverywhere.com/.

Ubersuggest[48] was created by renowned digital marketing strategist and author Neil Patel, because he felt that aspiring digital marketers should have a free keyword research tool they could trust. It is touted by many marketers as a great way to get keyword ideas for blog posts, and possibly provides even more ideas than Google's Keyword Planner.

Keyword Planner[49] has been the industry standard tool by which keyword research has been measured. It is a technically free keyword research tool embedded in a Google Ads (formerly Google AdWords). You will need to set up a Google Ads account to use it. While it costs money to run Google Ad campaigns, you can do keyword research with this tool without an active campaign running.

Twin Word[50] allows ten free searches a day. This tool provides similar data to those already described, but is known for helping you find patterns, and its filters allow you to customize how you want results displayed. One such filter shows User Intent in five categories to help you determine the intent your audience may have had when searching for a particular keyword. If the topic they intended to search for doesn't match up with what you're offering, you'll want to find other keyword options. (Find out more about how and **why you should consider user intent**[51].)

Google Search Console[52] has functionality that shows what keywords are leading users to your website, as well as light keyword research.

The tools below differ from true keyword research but can be very helpful for "informed brainstorming."

Answer the Public[53] is a tool best used for brainstorming rather than measuring search volume and competition ratios. It's effective for finding out what kind of questions people are asking about a certain topic. It's based on UK data, but the info is still relevant for content creators anywhere in the world.

Google Trends[54] allows you to compare two or more different topics to see which one is searched for most frequently.

Soovle[55] is a customizable engine that unites the suggestion phrases from all the major providers (Google, Bing, Amazon, Answers.com, Yahoo, Wikipedia, YouTube) in one place. This tool can be **a major help for search and content creation inspiration**[56].

48 "Ubersuggest's Free Keyword Tool, Generate More Suggestions." *Neil Patel*, 17 Apr. 2020, neilpatel.com/ubersuggest/.
49 "How to Use The Keyword Planner Tool." *Google Ads*, Google, ads.google.com/home/resources/using-google-ads-keyword-planner/.
50 "Keyword Tool Faster with AI." *Twinword Ideas*, www.twinword.com/ideas/.
51 Baadsgaard, Jacob, et al. "Intent-Based Keyword Research: Let Google Be Your Guide." *Search Engine Land*, 26 Apr. 2018, searchengineland.com/intent-based-keyword-research-let-google-be-your-guide-296795.
52 *Google Trends, Google*, trends.google.com/trends/?geo=US.
53 "Search Listening Tool for Market, Customer & Content Research." *AnswerThePublic*, answerthepublic.com/.
54 Google Trends, Google, trends.google.com/trends/?geo=US.
55 "Let the Web Help." *Soovle*, www.soovle.com/.
56 Smarty, Ann. "Soovle: Have Fun with Your Keywords." *Search Engine Journal*, Search Engine Journal, 17 Apr. 2010, www.searchenginejournal.com/soovle-have-fun-with-your-keywords/20053/.

YouTube has its own keyword research tools: **vidIQ**[57] and **TubeBuddy**[58]. Ubersuggest also has an option to look on YouTube.

5) Create content from keyword research.

Once you've utilized these tactics and tools, it's time to use this knowledge for your content planning. Keyword research does more than just tell you which words to use. It tells you which topics are popular, which topics are competitive, and what your best content opportunities may be.

This is good news! This means that the organizational methods you learned for writing essays and research papers in school will now pay off in a practical way. For blogs and websites, begin by writing an introduction to a topic (one webpage), then cover the topic (another webpage), then cover related topics (more separate webpages) or background information (another separate webpage or two). It's essentially writing an outline, and each section of the outline is a webpage. Blogs organized like this score highly in both search engine visibility and user-friendliness. For good examples of this, visit **sdadata.org/ seo**. From a visitor's perspective, this streamlines navigation within a specific topic. But, be careful not to take this concept to the extreme, creating a confusing maze of short pages.

Remember that relevant topics and strong topic coverage have a stronger influence on search engine ranking than using individual words or phrases repetitively. The algorithm rewards quality writing and presentation.

However, keywords do still matter!

Keyword research helps us know what words and phrases people are using. We still want to use those words and phrases as often as we can on a page—naturally. If it sounds hokey to keep repeating a phrase, find another way to say it that means the same thing. Overall, you still want the content to read as naturally and conversationally as possible, as if you were telling this information to a friend.

Here are some tips for thorough topic coverage in natural language that can be adapted for a variety of content types:

If you were telling your friend about Pathfinder knots because you'd done the research and knew they were interested in teaching this honor, you would certainly use the proper names of each knot, as well as some common nicknames or synonyms. The next steps would be to:

Provide context for how you learned to master each knot and highlight some parts of the learning process that were trickier than others.

Give advice regarding the best time to use one knot over others.

Highlight some common mistakes people make when trying to determine which knot to use.

---

57 "How To Get More Views And Subscribers On YouTube." *VidIQ*, vidiq.com/.
58 TubeBuddy. "The Premier YouTube Channel Management and Optimization Toolkit." TubeBuddy, www.tubebuddy.com/.

Then, if you had a rope and video camera (or smart phone), you'd do a demonstration to sum up the main ideas and conclude that knot-tying is important and that the reason so many knots exist is because they all serve a unique purpose.

After that, you might ask if your friend had any questions.

Work your way through a topic, creating as much applicable content as possible over multiple digital media posts and platforms. Content organization techniques that may help you include outlines, topic trees, bubble graphs, etc. Using these as your foundation for content creation helps you determine topical goals, objectives, and key takeaways, and makes the whole writing process easier.

Content Evangelism: Engaging Your Audience and Improving SEO

When it comes to digital evangelism and discipleship, content is made to inform, to educate, and inspire—for the purpose of attracting and nurturing a loyal audience that connects with your ministry's message. Ultimately, your goal is to support their growth in their spiritual journey.

The currency of content marketing (or in our case, evangelism) is ACT: Authority, Credibility, and Trustworthiness (though we should also add "Empathy" to this list, especially when dealing with spiritual topics and life lessons).

Use multiple forms of content to maximize your organization's ability to get picked up by Google's search algorithms, as well as to further engage your audience. Keep in mind that certain forms of content will perform better with some audiences than others. By diversifying your content creation strategy, you optimize your reach and increase your impact across a variety of demographics.

Here are the four major components that work together in a comprehensive content creation process[59]:

> **Strategy** – defining your ministry's purpose, goals, and niche opportunities to target. Effective strategies outline topic coverage and evaluate means of distribution, measurement, and analysis.

> **Copy** – the words within the content. What messages are being conveyed to your audience? How can the language best reflect the culture of the medium and the target audience so that the desired meaning can be best understood? Remember, good communication is when we speak so that our intended audience can not only hear our message, but understand its intended meaning or purpose.

> **Imagery** – the pictures, videos, icons, and graphics. What's your visual theme? What emotional response or mood are your trying to evoke? What perception(s) of your brand will your audience develop of your brand based on the images you utilize?

> **Medium/Media** – The final home(s) for the copy and imagery content. Where will it live? On your website? In an app? On another website? On various social media platforms?

As you continue through this section, consider how each of the following elements will fit into the above four categories.

---

59 Schroeder, Britney, et al. "Types of Content Marketing: Power Digital Marketing." *Power Digital*, 2 July 2019, powerdigitalmarketing.com/blog/different-types-of-content-marketing/.

Most Popular Types of Online Content

Text

The written word is the foundation of any type of content, and, therefore, this is where we must begin. Ideas are usually written down first—whether in the form of notes, scripts, or outlines—before they're turned into anything else. Even in visual media like video, written content often accompanies and supports the other content types. When you set your content evangelism goals, you'll want to prioritize quality writing.

Keep in mind, however, that good writing in an academic sense is not the same as what's considered good content writing or copywriting. Writing for digital environments is much more straightforward, casual, conversational, and concise.

The most common forms of written content online are:

Website copy, as in, the text found throughout your organization or ministry website. A thorough outline or bubble diagram is a must for planning out website content. Each page should have a clear purpose made obvious in the headline and introductory sentences. Typically, you'll start with writing copy for the following standard pages: "Home," "About," "Services," and "Contact Us." You'll expand from there, depending on your type of ministry.

The more high-quality content your website has, the more likely it is to show up in search results for topics related to your mission—especially if it has a blog.

Blogs[60], or a consistently-updated collection of topical articles. The word "blog" originally came from the word "weblog," back when blogs were more like online journals for individuals posting their opinions or recipes, documenting their parenting journey, etc. Now blogs are used both individually and commercially to engage in conversation and as a means to inform (or persuade) readers.

Many blogs have inspired the formation of online communities, especially if they prominently link to their corresponding social media profiles on Instagram, YouTube, Facebook, Twitter, etc. Many commercial websites also leverage blogs to build or grow a community around brand values. **If an organization's blog contains useful or thought-provoking information, and is properly promoted**[61], it can skyrocket in online influence. Often, this also increases audience conversions (taking a desired action).

Landing pages, or a stand-alone page dedicated to one important message, campaign, and/or call-to-action. It's more than just a page where users happen to "land" after a search. Landing pages are where visitors are directed via a website link, social media post, paid advertising campaign, email button, etc., for the purpose of

---

60 Rowse, Darren. "4 Reasons Why You Should Start a Blog in the New Year." *ProBlogger*, 9 Jan. 2020, problogger.com/how-to-start-a-blog-in-the-new-year/.

61 Elias, Benyamin. "How to Write a Perfect Blog Post." 8 *Formatting Tips to Craft a Great Post*, ActiveCampaign, 28 Oct. 2019, www.activecampaign.com/blog/how-to-write-a-perfect-blog-post.

taking a specific action. A landing page is where a visitor would be directed to learn about a specific campaign, cause, or opportunity, and is designed to encourage them to get involved or sign-up for a special offer. The call-to-action would ask them to enter an email address (or other additional information) in exchange for something like:

o   a subscription to your newsletter on marriage

o   registration for a webinar or upcoming event on healthy eating

o   the opportunity to sign up to meet with a local Bible worker or pastor

o   a "lead magnet," such as a free e-book (or physical book) on a topic of interest, such as "What happens when we die?"

The primary purpose of landing pages should be to gather email addresses and other contact information for your marketing list, as well as analytic data on how many people are interested in what you're offering. With the right promotional strategy, landing pages are valuable tools for growing your digital influence.

Landing pages can also help your organization increase registrations, sign-ups, downloads, purchases, etc. When applicable, build in "buzz" words that create a sense of urgency or exclusivity that urge visitors to take action or that make them feel special.

Email content. Email marketing[62] is still a key player when it comes to optimizing your digital influence. While this content is not indexed by search engines, it serves a vital function in nurturing the relationship your ministry builds with its audience. It helps to grow an actively engaged digital following across multiple mediums and platforms, which does boost your SEO.

However, for your message to have an impact, your audience must first open your email. Strategically written subject lines are meant to convince the reader to open your email. And once they do, the email content should be written as concisely and in as straightforward a manner as possible, as you only have a matter of seconds to engage the reader and pique their interest.

Most email marketing content is in the form of e-newsletters that keep your community informed on news, events, resources, new content, etc. Emails may be notifications of new blog posts, or sometimes email campaigns can be an educational series in and of themselves.

Think about what you get in your inbox. Maybe you're on an email list that sends you a daily devotional. Whatever type of email you receive, understand that careful thought (hopefully) went into how that content was presented. Email content is intentionally designed to keep readers engaged and feeling special so they don't wander down to the footer to click "unsubscribe."

---

62 "A Beginner's Guide to Successful Email Marketing." *Neil Patel*, 24 Jan. 2020, neilpatel.com/blog/beginners-guide-email-marketing/.

Testimonials. This content features member/participant stories and testimonies that promote your mission, message, event, or cause. Storytelling remains central to evangelism because we're drawn to the narrative of someone "just like us" experiencing a problem, seeking the right solution, trying this and trying that, and finally discovering how to overcome the problem.

Testimonials allow your ministry to be the "great discovery," demonstrating that it can help people succeed and find a happy ending to their story. Around the testimonial, you can highlight your mission, what your ministry provides that others don't, and give people a glimpse of what their lives would be like if they embraced your ideas or joined your faith community.

E-books. E-books educate readers (provide value) about a topic of interest. For an audience that might be looking for more depth, an e-book is a good option for going deeper than a blog or social media post allows. E-books can be terrific lead magnets as well. You can use landing pages to encourage people to sign up to receive e-books as well as physical books.

Social media posts. Many organizations assign their best writers to engage with their followers on Twitter, Instagram, Facebook, LinkedIn, and various niche-specific platforms. Social media writing requires short, punchy messaging that encourages discussion, inspires shares, or includes an enticing call-to-action that directs to a landing page, blog, registration page, full video, etc. We'll discuss more about how to write effectively for social media and online audiences in the next section.

Social media is today's "word of mouth." It's the central hub of online conversations, and, if they want their posts read, liked, and shared, social media writers need to write in the word-of-mouth style, catering to the audience's interests, frustrations, and convictions, and using strong, specific calls-to-action.

Social media "buzz" can dramatically increase your ministry's web presence and impact. Not only is it a good source of active backlinks that can drive traffic to your website, your social media profiles can appear as additional search results as well—further elevating your findability online.

SEO titles and tags, such as page titles, headlines (or H1s), **meta descriptions**[63] (the intro blurb that appears underneath the page title and link in search results), and ALT tags. All of these are priorities for SEO copywriters, as the content found in these areas can make a big difference in which webpages get clicked on and ranked in search results.

Microcontent, or "scannable web copy[64]**,"** which refers to headlines, subtitles, subheaders, lists, pull quotes, sidebars, meta descriptions, calls-to-action, etc. **These**

---

63 "SEO Basics: Breakdown and Summary Check-List." *Digital Evangelism*, www.sdadata.org/digital-evangelism-blog/seo-basics-breakdown-and-summary-check-list.

64 Sorrentino, Dominick, and Dominick Sorrentino. "Micro Content: What Is It and Why Do You Need It?" *Brafton*, 25 July 2018, www.brafton.com/blog/creation/microcontent-what-is-it-and-why-do-you-need-it/.

are very important[65], and it's actually an area that demands the most creativity from the writer. Its purpose is to make content more scannable, overcoming the "wall of text" issue that deters so many potential readers. More often than not, the microcontent is what convinces a reader to start reading and to keep reading.

Transcripts for videos or podcasts. Some sites post them verbatim, while others optimize them for readability and add microcontent. This can make the transcript just as popular as the recording, especially for those (**about 16% of web users**[66]) that prefer to read content. It is also highly valuable for making the content of the recording indexable for search engines. It is also a good way to promote accessibility for users that use screen-readers. Accessible content is valued by search engines.

Checklists, as they can stand alone as their own type of post. They can appeal to hurried readers who love scannability, and to thorough readers who like the idea of a concrete list they can check off as they apply each step. Detailed checklists can also be effective lead magnets to the right audience, especially if your content teaches a complex process or provides ways to improve an existing skill or behavior.

Video

One-third[67] of all online activity is spent watching video. This isn't surprising. People, as visual creatures, have been naturally drawn to online video and made it one of the most popular ways to consume content **for all ages**[68]! The increase in mobile device usage has made video more popular as well. With a smaller screen, it's easier and faster to watch videos than to read text.

Video is a great enhancer. Have you noticed that when you click on a news story, the page often has both the written article and the video from the newscast? Not only does it offer two different options for content consumption, it adds a perception of depth and authority to the story.

Video content is particularly useful for educational topics, especially "how-to" tutorials and telling stories. Demonstrations, interviews, personal testimonies, time-lapses...some things are just better presented via video.

When it comes to **YouTube**, this platform has created its own niche of search engine optimization. YouTube's search algorithms rely heavily on keywords, titles, tags, thumbnail images, and microcontent such as video descriptions and channel descriptions.

YouTube also measures "watch time," or how long a viewer watches before clicking away or going back to search results. The more of a video that gets watched, the better that

65 Sorrentino, Dominick, and Dominick Sorrentino. "Micro Content: What Is It and Why Do You Need It?" *Brafton*, 25 July 2018, www.brafton.com/blog/creation/microcontent-what-is-it-and-why-do-you-need-it/.

66 "Why Scannable Web Copy?" *Wylie's Writing Tips*, 15 May 2018, freewritingtips.wyliecomm.com/2018-05-15/.

67 "37 Staggering Video Marketing Statistics for 2018." *WordStream*, www.wordstream.com/blog/ws/2017/03/08/video-marketing-statistics.

68 Olenski, Steve. "Why Brands Marketing To Baby Boomers Need To Use Video." *Forbes*, Forbes Magazine, 26 July 2018, www.forbes.com/sites/steveolenski/2018/07/25/why-brands-marketing-to-baby-boomers-need-to-use-video/#175dddb4da6f.

video must be, so YouTube ranks it higher in its search results. Longer videos, especially if frequently watched until the end, get even more of a boost (on other social media platforms, however, it is still generally recommended to keep videos short, around three to five minutes or less).

Livestreams

With livestreaming, longer videos are always acceptable, regardless of platform. Livestreaming your events, whether on Facebook Live, YouTube, or your website, can widen your audience, further engage your existing audience, and provide an archivable piece of evergreen content that can be repurposed later. This is great for church services, special performances, programs at a school or university, conference sessions, and more.

When it comes to SEO, livestreams can have a sizeable effect. Facebook **announced**[69] that its ranking algorithm favors live videos in its searches. YouTube promotes YouTube Live videos. And even if your organization's livestreams are hosted off-site, it's another link to your content that could show up in search results—especially if you're live often!

Webinars (Online training or Bible studies)

Taking video up another notch, webinars are exclusive, live, educational presentations. Like its name suggests, it's a seminar broadcast over the web using tools such as **GoToMeeting**, **Zoom**, or **Lifesize**. Participants are typically invited to webinars and provided with a private link.

While the webinar itself would not be indexed by search engines, its power to engage audiences boosts SEO through lead generation and by increasing engagement, trust, and loyalty to your ministry. Webinars can provide a valuable service to your constituents when used to teach useful information (such as tips to improve your marriage), provide background on a popular issue, or facilitate live online discussions. They can also be an effective and convenient way to host digital Bible studies for small groups, allowing face-to-face interaction and relationship building regardless of location.

Images

While the right pictures can elicit emotion, the right designs can inspire action and highlight strategic details. Careful planning is necessary to make sure the images you've chosen indeed emphasize the intended emotion. It must be clear what the picture is portraying, and it should look genuine, as opposed to a cliché corporate **stock photo**.

Used sparingly, stock photography can be a great resource to enhance your ministry's brand online, and it's easy to find free stock images at **pixabay**, **pexels**, **unsplash**, and **free-images.com**.

---

69 "Taking into Account Live Video When Ranking Feed." *About Facebook*, 7 Nov. 2019, about.fb.com/news/2016/03/news-feed-fyi-taking-into-account-live-video-when-ranking-feed/.

For websites, **hero images** (the large, single images that dominate the top area of a website) continue to be trending. These pictures must be high enough resolution to avoid appearing pixelated (approx. 1600 pixels wide), but low enough resolution to avoid slowing down the site's load time.

For other images that appear on your website, stick to file sizes under 250 kilobytes if possible.

For each image on your website, blog, or Instagram profile, make sure to apply **ALT text**[70], which is indexed by search engines to determine what the picture is about. It also acts as text that can be read by screen readers to tell visually-impaired internet users what pictures are on a page.

Infographics

When explaining a process in text, an accompanying visual is a must.

If, when talking about your topic, you find yourself saying, "Here, let me show you..." or, "Why don't I just draw this out," an infographic would probably come in handy.

Infographics illustrate each step or point of a process and include short and straightforward text to accompany the imagery—making complicated information easier to understand.

Designers and writers must work closely to create an infographic with a clear direction so the eye knows what to read first and where to go next.

If you're short a graphic designer, some free tools like Canva can help you create simple infographics, which add a splash of color to your page, post, or feed while informing and engaging your audience in a creative way.

Infographics don't just make your page more pleasant to look at—people actually search for infographics on certain topics. They're also shared frequently on social media. Think of creative ways to use infographics for ministry, such as mapping out "How to Study the Bible for Beginners.[71]

Podcasts

Audio content can include interviews, sermons, vocal essays, monologues, presentations, seminars, and more. Podcasts created from this audio content should be distributed as widely as possible, including on your website, iTunes, and other hosting platforms so users can subscribe. Even if you're already hosting through a provider such as **SoundCloud**, **Blubrry**, **Google Drive**, or **archive.org**, it's worth uploading to other hosting platforms in addition. These simple audio files are a highly shareable piece of content people can listen to while driving, walking, exercising, or cleaning their garage.

---

70 "Alt Text for Images - Examples & 2020 Best Practices." *Moz*, moz.com/learn/seo/alt-text.

71 1 *https://www.impactbnd.com/hs-fs/hubfs/onespot-infographic-about-infographics.jpg*

Having podcasts with your ministry's name in the title, or hosted by a prominent personality associated with your ministry, can do wonders for brand awareness, which ultimately benefits overall SEO.

Interactive content (quizzes, polls, calculators, etc.)

This type of content requires audience participation, making their interaction with your ministry far more memorable.

You've probably seen various character quizzes on Facebook or Twitter. They are highly shareable because, to the audience, it feels like they're sharing information about themselves, not about the organization that designed the quiz.

Interactive content[72] that strives to be helpful or practical might include assessment-type quizzes, calculators, interactive graphs or charts, or polls and surveys. They can also help you with demographic info-gathering for your ministry's strategic planning. Remember, anything that deepens engagement also boosts SEO! It's always beneficial to keep people on your website longer.

There are many tools that can help you create interactive content, including **qzzr**, **SurveyMonkey**, **Doodle**, **Vizia**, and more.

Courses

This type of content can be important for building what Google refers to as an organization's E-A-T (Expertise, Authority, Trustworthiness). At the same time, courses provide yet another way for your audience to consume your content. If your organization is qualified to teach even a simple skill that has value in your audience's life (healthy cooking or practical discipleship tips), creating courses can bolster your content marketing and SEO, and become a relevant resource for your site visitors. Not only can this type of content boost your credibility, it can empower your audience for positive change.

Beginning Content Strategy Worksheet

Filling out this structural worksheet can guide your brainstorming process and help you solidify your content strategy.

1. Which topics do you wish to cover in-depth for your content evangelism?

---

72 Bullock, Lilach, et al. "10 Best Tools to Create Interactive Content." *LilachBullock*, 1 Oct. 2019, www.lilachbullock.com/interactive-content-tools/.

2. What goals and objectives do you have for your content evangelism?

3. What keywords relate to your topic? Brainstorm below.

4. Run your topic and keyword ideas through a keyword research tool. What kinds of results do you find?

5. Are the terms you thought would be popular showing high search volume?

6. Which keywords show the most favorable ratio of search volume to competition?

7. Using what you've determined from your keyword research, what is the main topic that will guide your content development?

8. List a few substantial subtopics that can branch out from your main topic.

9. Create a "topic tree" or bubble diagram to outline your content's topical progression.

10. What possible content titles come to mind? Brainstorm below.

11. For which of these subtopics would it be most useful to invest in a visual element, such as a video, infographic, or image?

12. Which platforms best suit these topics and/or content types? Which platforms would best reach your target audience?

13. Start drafting content assignments and/or a publishing schedule, include guidelines for visual content, and describe the places and forms it will be published in. Even the best writers must adapt their style for online writing.

Writing Effectively for Online Audiences

Even the best writers must adapt their style for online writing.

While learning the rules and best practices of academic or journalistic writing creates a solid educational foundation, online writing requires a completely different style and approach to get the point across as quickly, clearly, and effectively as possible.

Copy that's written for an online audience may seem too simple, even formulaic, since this type of writing is more casual and straight-forward. However, years of research proves its effectiveness in the digital space.

Bottom line: the goal of writing online content is to connect with the reader, not elevate the author. It's about meeting the reader where they are and giving them the information they seek, all while "desiring their good" (**sound familiar? MH, 143[73]**).

In other words, it's not about us; it's about those we are seeking to serve. As you read through this section, remember:

Writing for an online audience is not the time to communicate in a way that highlights the author's vocabulary or intelligence. Our goal is always to uplift Christ first, and this means putting self aside in all aspects of ministry and prioritizing the needs of those we serve. We should endeavor to meet people where they are, on the platforms where they spend their time, in the way they prefer to consume content, and with language they can connect with.

Good communication is when you communicate in a way your audience understands.

---

73 "The Ministry of Healing." - *Ellen G. White Writings*, m.egwwritings.org/en/book/135.635.

9 PRINCIPLES FOR WRITING STRONG ONLINE CONTENT

1) Remember the primary purposes for online writing (content evangelism).

Effective online writing has at least one of the following primary goals. This is especially true for content marketing/evangelism, which requires consistent production and distribution of quality content to attract, engage, and nurture an audience.

The purposes are:

To inform your readers about a topic of interest, providing new information—or old information—with a unique twist, new application, or original perspective. Aimed at providing value, this type of content makes the reader feel like they've become more knowledgeable because of engaging with your content.

To educate your readers with answers to their questions or solutions to their problems. This can demonstrate authority while also providing a service to your audience. Most educational article titles start with "How" or "How to" or "Learn." You can also use videos, quizzes, courses, step-by-step guides, checklists, eBooks, white papers, handbooks, reports, and more to provide your audience with educational content.

To entertain people who are searching for something lighthearted to pass the time, or who need a pick-me-up. This type of content can even inform or educate in a fun way, but without demanding too much brainpower. Entertaining content is often viewed while on a commute (when the reader is not the driver!), in waiting rooms, between classes, on breaks at work, while waiting for an event to start, or on the couch, winding down after a long day. Here you'll want to utilize forms of content such as quizzes, games, polls, short videos, memes, or humorous writing.

To inspire your readers to take an action, such as changing a habit, sharing a post, registering for your event, signing up for a free resource, supporting your cause, or donating. Inspiring content targets emotions, stirring up feelings of agitation which could be positive (excited, emboldened) or negative (angry, shocked). However, this type of content must be used carefully. Emotional content performs poorly if the reader perceives it to be overblown or insincere. Always strive to be realistic and authentic. When possible, first test your content on a smaller audience before scaling up the reach of your articles or posts.

2) Write like you're talking to a friend: conversationally.

The best online writing is conversational, yet straightforward. Think about how you'd explain something new to someone you know, and write just like you would speak (minus tics, fillers, and mannerisms).

You wouldn't waste time on flowery, poetic words, and you'd try to relate your concept to your friend's life. You'd be up front about why this subject might be of interest and how it could benefit them in particular. The number one reason people share content online is because they feel it will improve the lives of others. As digital evangelists, our goal should be to create sharable content that benefits the lives of others. The Church should be a leader in creating content of this kind.

In addition, you shouldn't spend a lot of time on technical details or bells and whistles, unless you know your friend is interested in that. Instead, you'd focus on how this topic will affect them personally.

The great part of writing targeted online content is that, as long as you're clear about your topic, your demographic will already be interested in what you're writing about! After all, they have searched for topics mentioned in your articles or posts and decided your page is worth visiting.

Since your readers used a search engine, social media post, email message, or other website to get to your content, you don't have to worry about convincing them that the topic itself is interesting. Your job is to convince them that you have information about their chosen topic that is better, deeper, more interesting, or more applicable than other sources. Ask yourself: what will the reader get from my content that they can't get from someone else?

Getting to your point early—in the headline, subtitle, and opening paragraph—is key.

Think about that conversation with a friend. Have you ever been in a conversation where your counterpart struggled to get to the point?

They're over-explaining the peripheral details, giving too many examples or metaphors, or trying to come up with language that softens the blow of an edgy idea or uncomfortable topic instead of outright saying what they mean.

You'd quickly realize how much time is being wasted and you'll wish you had asked someone else to begin with!

That's how an online reader feels when the content doesn't get to the point.

They'll click "back" and go to the next link in the search results.

Tips for writing conversationally

Use:

- simple, easy-to-understand language.
- words with fewer syllables. Words with more syllables reduce readability.
- "you," "your," and "I." This makes it seem like you're speaking to your audience personally.
- active voice instead of passive voice.
- examples, similes, and metaphors (but don't go overboard).
- contractions.

Be sure to:

- tell stories. These are easy to remember and more engaging.
- keep it short and digestible. Break long sentences into several short ones. Long sentences will reduce readability. Blog posts, for example, should be no more than 800-1,200 words.
- ask questions.
- write to your target audience.

And, finally:

- do not ramble.

Fancy, academic writing doesn't work for digital media. Aim to write simply, honestly, and conversationally.

3) Evoke an emotional response.

Reaching your target audiences in a deep and emotionally compelling way is key to effective communication, powerful evangelism (marketing), and creating authentic connections. In the case of mission work and cause-based initiatives, strategic placement of key words can help facilitate deeper thought and increase impact on the reader, driving them to action.

The best headlines and teaser lines receive an "Emotional Marketing Value" (EMV) score of over 40. In other words, the best online writing incorporates high impact words in a way that is quickly understood by the reader and evokes an emotional response. We are after all, highly emotional beings, who often make decisions based on what directly affects us. In a world of competing priorities and overwhelming need, this can be a useful tool to help your message stand out among the digital clutter. Afterall, your message must be read in order to have impact.

The emotional richness of copy is evaluated based on three categories

Intellectual	Empathetic	Spiritual
Words which are effective when offering products and services that require reasoning or careful evaluation.	Words which bring out profound and strong positive emotional reactions in people.	Words which have the strongest potential for influence and often appeal to people at a very deep emotional level.

Source: *aminstitute.com/headline*

Gorgeous2God example: Life is tough but you're not alone. Join our community of young Christian women tackling real issues from a godly perspective.

- **EMV = 42.86%**

Seminar Example: Feeling defeated? Marriage is hard and you're struggling. We're here for you. Join us for a free seminar. Click here to register in advance and get a free book with 5 practical tips for improving your marriage.

- **EMV = 50%** for "Feeling defeated? Marriage is hard and you're struggling. We're here for you. Join us for a free seminar."

Visit **aminstitute.com/headline** to learn more and check the EMV score of your messages and headlines.

Remember to also boldly make your claim up front, then use the rest of your content to back it up. If the point you're making is a bit jarring, that's not necessarily a bad thing. Plus, by getting to the point early, you tell your audience why they should prioritize your content over someone else's. People are busy; state the value up front and then deliver on that promise.

Consider the idea of inspiring people by agitating emotional states:

> *"People don't do things because they're comfortable. People don't do things because they're bored. People do things because they're excited, outraged, empowered, inspired, shocked..."* —Christofer Jeschke

Example: Feeling depressed? You're not alone. 10 ways a relationship with Jesus will dramatically improve your life.

- **EMV = 50%**

Example: You know probably someone who has been abused. You CAN do something. Learn the signs and red flags. Know what to do.

- **EMV = 45%**

We're emotional beings, and the most effective writing tugs at these emotions without going overboard and *without being manipulative or sensational*.

4) Move your reader to action.

The heart of **copywriting**[74] is persuading readers to take an action.

Sometimes, when we think of marketing copy, we think about those spammy e-mail subject lines that over-promise and over-guarantee, or we cringe at clickbait headlines for videos or blog posts.

Well, if sales copy puts a bad taste in your mouth, keep in mind that you're thinking of *bad* sales copy. **When copywriting is done conversationally**[75], with the reader's feelings, interests, and beliefs/core values in mind, it can be incredibly effective. Remember, people are drawn to authenticity and honesty. Church messaging should always demonstrate the highest level of integrity.

Define the problem

Throughout a piece of writing, a reader is moved to action by **introducing a problem that the reader needs to solve**[76]. They want something, they're confused about something, or they don't know the next step in a process.

You outline the problem, describe the implications of this problem, and then give them the solution—your resource, your solution, your method, your information, etc.

Benefits vs. features

When describing how great your resources/belief/method/service/information is, don't just list its features—describe the benefits it will provide to your reader, and why those benefits are in their best interest. People want to know why before they take the time to understand the how.

---

74 "Copywriting 101: How to Craft Compelling Copy." *Copyblogger*, 21 Feb. 2019, copyblogger.com/copywriting-101/.
75 Usborne, Nick UsborneNick, et al. "3 False Beliefs about Conversational Copywriting That Make Me Want to Scream." *Copyblogger*, 3 Apr. 2018, copyblogger.com/conversational-copywriting/.
76 Weaver, Belinda, et al. "Classic Copywriting Formula: Problem-Agitate-Solve Oh My!" *Copywrite Matters*, 18 July 2019, copywritematters.com/pas-classic-copywriting-formula/.

For example:

"Buy our hibiscus tea!"

Why?

"Our blend has more antioxidants."

Ok...what does that mean?

"Antioxidants decrease free radicals in your bloodstream."

Ok...what does that mean?

"Antioxidants keep the cells in your body from breaking down!"

Ok...but what does that mean for me?

"Well, this tea has been shown to help lower high blood pressure, according to the American Heart Association's 2008 study."

That sounds pretty important. How does it taste?

"Great! Especially with honey!"

Well, all right then—why didn't you say so?

When we're personally invested in the subject of our writing, we can get lost in the details. Remember that the readers aren't there yet. They need to see a connection between what they're searching for and what you have to offer.

For example:

"You've been diagnosed with high blood pressure, and it can be tough to give up some of the foods and beverages you've enjoyed for years—like coffee, black tea, and soda."

You speak the truth. It's like you've been there, man!

"But what if there was a soothing hot drink that could be just as tasty, AND help lower your blood pressure at the same time?"

Is there? That would be so helpful right now! Tell me more!

Superperfect Tea Company offers premium hibiscus tea. And, according to a 2008 study by the American Heart Association, it lowers blood pressure in pre-hypertensive and mildly hypertensive adults.

I could use that! How does it taste?

This ruby-red herbal tea has a slight tart flavor reminiscent of cranberries. Add a little honey, and it delivers a light, tangy "bite" that can pick you up in the afternoon or calm you down in the evening.

Mmm. Can I try some?

Notice how the problem was outlined in the introduction, with the primary benefits immediately following. Meet the readers where they are, then tell how your amazing product is just what they need...and why.

Now, if we frame this in the context of ministry, your product is your message, which may be hope, wholeness, health, lifestyle, truth that answers their deepest longing, answers to their physical/spiritual needs, sound advice, and more.

Calls-to-action (CTA)

Once you've "sold" the product by connecting with your readers' needs, it's time to tell them to buy it! In ministry, this may mean subscribing to your newsletter, registering for a seminar or health clinic, coming to an event, or joining a small group dedicated to a particular topic.

Don't leave them hanging. They want to take action, and the more clear and straightforward the call, the more likely they are to follow through.

You may have already imagined a call-to-action following the last line of the hibiscus tea conversation:

"Yes! Get 20% off your first box of tea when you order now!"

or

"Yes—get a free sample sent to you now!"

Copywriting isn't complete without a call-to-action. It doesn't have to be overly clever or cute; it just needs to make sense. Here are the most common calls to action that appear in online marketing:

- Order now!
- Download here.
- Watch this video.
- Join today!
- Donate to [insert organization name] & get a free travel mug!
- Listen now!
- Register now and get a free [insert item]!

- Start your free trial today!
- Secure your spot!
- Get the full version!
- Access exclusive information!
- Sponsor a child today!
- Book your appointment now!
- Find out if you qualify!

5) Tell stories.

To share stories is human and approachable.

> *There is an old Jewish parable of "Truth & Story" where naked Truth traveled from village to village trying to find acceptance and love. In each village, Truth was mocked, ridiculed and ultimately chased away. Naked Truth was hated by all she encountered. From afar, Truth saw Story, dressed in beautiful robes, enter the village that had just rejected her. The people loved Story and praised her beauty, quickly embracing her. Story later found Truth crying far outside the village and asked what was wrong. Truth revealed her desire to be accepted like Story and shared the pain of her experiences. Taking pity upon Truth, Story shared some of her beautiful robes with her so that she was no longer naked. From then on, Truth and Story always traveled together, and everywhere they went, the people rejoiced and welcomed them.*

Storytelling is a powerful means of communication online because:

> *Stories never tell us what to think, they give us something to think about. Stories don't tell us what to feel, they cause us to feel.*

Effective writing is both a science and an art. Yes, wordsmithing is a creative process, but copywriting is a science backed by research. A great way to add creativity to the elements of formulaic copywriting is through storytelling. People can't help but be interested in stories. As humans, we want to know how things turn out!

For generations, storytelling has been the way people learn their history and connect. The Bible itself can be viewed as a collection of stories that draw people to God, teach us difficult truths, and connect us through a shared set of beliefs. To "win" souls, we, as a Church, must connect with a person's experiences through stories. Not only is storytelling a powerful means of communication, but a vital tool for sharing a message of hope. Jesus told parables because truths revealed through stories are an effective way to reach people with thought-provoking topics that are easy to remember. We, like Jesus, should become expert storytellers.

Storytelling connects people and gets them engaged and interested in each other. The reason why people love watching movies and reading books is because we love to be immersed in stories. Social media is people connecting with people to create a collective human story. Our job is to frame that story within the context of our faith. We can provide answers and connection online users are looking for, if we're strategic and intentional with what we write and the content we create.

Stories can be in the form of case studies, testimonials, video retellings, or simple anecdotes that describe how a person—just like the reader—struggled with a specific problem. Maybe they tried several things until finally discovering what really worked.

Where can you find real stories? As a ministry, you might already have them. Think of the people you've served. Think of the events you've held. Think of the testimonies your constituents have shared with you. How does their journey reflect a common need or experience within your target audience?

Going deeper, what analogies or metaphors can you draw from what you do? Can it be related to common daily life concerns? How does your ministry offer practical solutions?

Check out this **article on finding marketing stories in everyday life**[77].

Write down a story that you would share with your audience that could come across as relatable and relevant to their core values or needs.

_____

_____

_____

_____

_____

_____

_____

_____

6) Know the difference between content writing and copywriting.

While these terms are sometimes used interchangeably, they are different. Copywriting refers to the science, the persuasive writing formulas, the headlines, and the calls-to-action. Content writing could be considered the filler content that fleshes out the formulas for content marketing purposes: the stories, the details, the background information, the educational steps, or other valuable pieces of information you're offering your reader.

In many ways these two elements of writing overlap and work together, and both occupy vital roles in the digital evangelism process.

There are increasingly specific definitions of these two terms across the internet, but the bottom line is that these writing styles and formulas work together to provide value to the reader, persuading them to stick around and, eventually, take action.

---

77 Robson, Heather. "Finding Marketing Stories in Your Everyday Life By Heather Robson." *American Writers & Artists Institute*, www.awai.com/2017/11/finding-marketing-stories-in-your-everyday-life/.

7) Know how to use evergreen vs. time-sensitive content.

There are two primary categories to consider when crafting your overall website content: time-sensitive content and evergreen content.

While, indeed, simple concepts, when it comes to SEO, content marketing, and user experience, there are strategies to consider in the implementation of these two content types.

Announcements, breaking news, special offers or promotions, seasonal content, and events are time sensitive by nature. It's good to have some time-sensitive information on your website and social media—if you consistently keep it up to date. It demonstrates to site visitors that your organization is active and aware.

It is more frustrating to go to a website/profile with out-of-date information than to go to a website/profile with no time-sensitive information at all. If an event from a couple months ago is still headlining, how can the visitor trust that the rest of your information is current?

Evergreen content, however, refers to elements on your page without an expiration date. It's static content that doesn't change (much) over time. It doesn't need to. It's written to stay relevant and useful to your audience regardless of when they read it.

For general website and social media copy, this evergreen content includes:

- About
- Services
- FAQ
- Archived posts or **cornerstone articles**[78]
- Resources
- Testimonials

Special care should be taken when creating this copy so it will stay relevant for as long as possible with minimal upkeep.

Effective messaging, whether you are publishing content regularly on a blog, posting on social media, or sending emails, requires new, helpful content to stay fresh and up to date. However, that doesn't mean that each piece of content must be time-sensitive. You can cultivate them to be evergreen as well as timely.

To keep new content evergreen, the key is to stick with topics rather than dates.

While some of your social media or email content may contain time-sensitive information, they can link back to an evergreen blog post that covers a related topic thoroughly and that you periodically update as information changes.

78 Wildwood, LynLyn. "The Complete Guide to Cornerstone Content for Your Blog in 2019." *AlienWP*, 16 Jan. 2019, alienwp. com/cornerstone-content/.

To help your posts, pages, and articles stay evergreen in SERPs (search engine results pages), try removing the publication date from your post (unless it's necessary). For the many seekers that check the date on webpages before clicking on them in search results, removing the date altogether can help present your content as timeless.

If you're a church posting each week's sermons as videos or podcasts, the first priority to keep these elements evergreen is to title each one topically rather than with the date of the service (i.e., "Teaching Your Kids to Pray" vs. "Sermon 4-25-17 on Prayer"). Note that you can still show the date in the subtitle or descriptions for members that search by date, but the title should be presented like a headline.

The topics covered in evergreen content must be "enduring topics," discussing common experiences of the human condition (job interview best practices, dealing with grief and loss), timeless skills (how to pray, how to change a tire) or opinion/discussion pieces (which translation of the Bible is best?, is it better to exercise in the morning or evening?).

Additional ideas for effective evergreen content with examples:

- **Case studies** ("How Pathfinders Made Me More Confident")
- **Day-in-the-life posts or videos** ("Shadowing a Pathfinder Director at Oshkosh")
- **Interviews** ("Joe Smith, Pathfinder Leader for 40 Years, Tells Us His Best Stories")
- **Adapted livestreams** ("Pathfinder Leadership Training—What Not to Do Skit")
- **Demonstration videos** ("Advanced Knot Tying")
- **Topical blog post** ("7 Ways to Deal With Rambunctious Kids")
- **Topical blog series** ("Getting the Most Out of Oshkosh, Part 1 of 3")

8) Find ways of repurposing content to diversify your presence across multiple platforms and channels.

We've covered the different types of content that can be created to reach a variety of content consumers, as well as what makes content "evergreen," or relevant past its publication date.

These principles can come in handy in the beginning stages of your SEO and content evangelism strategy and when it comes to repurposing content. Instead of creating a different piece of content for each platform you publish to, you can repurpose one core content piece to work across a variety of channels.

Here's an example of how you can make one blog post explode into ten different pieces of shareable content:

You, a nationally-renowned sandwich artist, wrote a winning post for your sandwich-making fans.

- **Publish blog post on your website:** "5 Creative Ways to Slice Sandwiches for Dazzling Hors D'oeuvres Trays."
- **Create teasers** for your blog post for your followers on:
  o **Facebook**
  o **Twitter**
  o **Instagram**
  o **Pinterest**
  o **etc.**
- Create an **infographic**, illustrating the step-by-step process of each fancy slicing technique.
- Put together a **slide deck** for further details on each step of sandwich-slicing artistry.
- Announce this fantastic post to your **email list**.
  o You could even create an exclusive **autoresponder series** (emails sent automatically to a mailing list based on specific rules/or subscriber behavior at defined intervals) that focuses even more in-depth on each of the five sandwich slicing methods.
- Host a **webinar or a Facebook live video** about the five slicing strategies for aspiring sandwich artists, with Q&A afterward.
- Turn that webinar into an evergreen **video** that will live on your YouTube or Vimeo channel.
- Host a **podcast**, where you gather with a fellow sandwich aficionado or two and discuss these five slicing techniques.
- Type up **transcripts** of the podcast discussion for those who prefer to read.
- **Turn your feedback into more shareable content**. Are you getting lots of comments on your blog post, your social media channels, or your videos? Did anyone submit ideas or questions? Publish a follow-up post or video that showcases your followers' pictures of their own slicing results, blooper videos, or new discoveries. Or create a quick video to share tips about part of the third slicing method that your virtual protégés are having a tough time with.

Repurposing content can allow a specific topic to be discussed online longer by spreading out the publication of each repurposed item.

Furthermore, the same topic repurposed into ten different forms (example above) can create a bigger splash as it makes its online debut. This strategy creates more options for Google to index, increasing your chances of showing up prominently in search results, and it also allows your content to show up in the search engine results for various social media platforms as well.

9) Consider SEO-specific elements of online writing (Titles, Tags, and Descriptions).

While seemingly small, these more technical areas of online writing can make a big difference in how Google views your site and in convincing people to click on your webpages and content in search results.

Title Tags

Sometimes called the "SEO Title," this is the title that appears in search engines and what is displayed at the top of a browser tab when a reader opens your page.

```
local bible study groups                              ✕   🔍
```

🔍 All   🗐 News   🖼 Images   ▶ Videos   🔗 Shopping   ⋮ More   Settings   Tools

About 42,500,000 results (0.60 seconds)

www.communitybiblestudy.org

Adults - Community Bible Study   Title tag, or "SEO Title"

Looking for an adult **Bible study** in your community? Find a class ... This is followed by a 15-30 minute large **group** teaching given by a trained Teaching Director.

Day Classes · Evening Classes · Special Needs Adults · Young Adults

www.meetup.com › topics › biblestudy ▾

Bible Study groups | Meetup

Largest **Bible Study groups**. Orlando Area Christian Singles. 4,582 Singles | Orlando, USA. Christian Singles. 4,183 Members | Columbus, USA. SINGLEFAITH. Orange County Singles for Christ. Nashville Christian Singles. The NYC Christian Social **Group**. Single Life DFW | Cross City Singles. Money, Wealth and Business.

lifewaywomen.com › 2016/01/20 › bible-studies-near-... ▾

Bible Studies Near You - LifeWay Women

Jan 20, 2016 - Whether you meet with a church **group**, participate in an online study, ... an opportunity to connect with other women through **local Bible study**.

Be clear and straightforward about what your page content covers. If your page is about Bible studies, make sure those two words are in the first three words of the title. According to the SEO experts at Backlinko.com, Google "puts more weight" on words found at the beginning of title tags.

For example, say you want to rank for the keyword/phrase "couples Bible study" and you thought of two SEO Title choices:

1) Weekly Couples Bible Study - ThisTown Church

2) Looking for a Bible study that caters to new couples?

Google would rank the first one over the second one because it would deem it more relevant and topic-centric. The second one is not a bad headline (save it for your H1!) but Google favors SEO Titles that are more direct.

Editing your page title in HTML code looks like this:

```
<head>

    <title>THIS IS YOUR PAGE TITLE</title>

</head>
```

Otherwise, most content management platforms have a designated space to add or change a webpage's title.

NOTE: If you already have significant traffic coming to your page with your current page title, even if it's not optimized for the intended keyword, you might want to check your analytics before changing it. If visitors that come in through that page are staying on your site and clicking, downloading, buying, etc., you may want to consider keeping it the same, because you don't want to lose that current traffic. If you notice that people are coming in through this page but then leaving the site, a title change could be highly beneficial.

Meta Tags or Meta Descriptions

This is the approximately 200-character teaser-like blurb that appears directly below the SEO title in search results. Often, this is what convinces the reader that your content is valuable.

Your meta description can be as long as you want, but Google will cut it off anywhere between 250-300 characters, depending on the amount of pixels those characters occupy.

While the recommendation used to be 160 characters, Google **raised the number**[79] of permitted characters as of December 2017. It was changed again in the spring of 2018, then later adjusted to the current recommendation of 200 characters. In light of this

---

79 Meyers, Peter J. "How Long Should Your Meta Description Be?" *Moz*, Moz, 16 Feb. 2019, moz.com/blog/how-long-should-your-meta-description-be-2018.

apparent state of flux, aim to keep meta tags as short as possible while including the necessary information.

---

local bible study groups	✕ 🔍

🔍 All   📰 News   🖼 Images   ▶ Videos   🔍 Shopping   ⋮ More   Settings   Tools

About 42,500,000 results (0.60 seconds)

www.communitybiblestudy.org

Adults - Community Bible Study   Meta Description

Looking for an adult **Bible study** in your community? Find a class ... This is followed by a 15-30 minute large **group** teaching given by a trained Teaching Director.

Day Classes · Evening Classes · Special Needs Adults · Young Adults

www.meetup.com › topics › biblestudy ▾

Bible Study groups | Meetup

Largest **Bible Study groups**. Orlando Area Christian Singles. 4,582 Singles | Orlando, USA. Christian Singles. 4,183 Members | Columbus, USA. SINGLEFAITH. Orange County Singles for Christ. Nashville Christian Singles. The NYC Christian Social **Group**. Single Life DFW | Cross City Singles. Money, Wealth and Business.

lifewaywomen.com › 2016/01/20 › bible-studies-near-... ▾

Bible Studies Near You - LifeWay Women

Jan 20, 2016 - Whether you meet with a church **group**, participate in an online study, ... an opportunity to connect with other women through **local Bible study**.

Using keywords in the meta description can give a small boost in search engine optimization, but the primary purpose of meta descriptions is to get the googler to click on your site. This is where you expand on your page title, pitching why your website has what they are looking for.

For example, if you're selling vegan, gluten-free granola bars, you might want your meta description to say something like:

> **VEGLUFRE—A fast, tasty, healthy breakfast option! Packed with protein, fiber, vitamins, and minerals, our vegan, gluten-free granola bars make a great meal or snack. 5 flavors! Order in bulk & save!**

Make sure to connect the benefits of your product, service, or idea/cause with the needs and interests of those you hope will click on your link. List a key selling point or two, then describe what they'll find on the page and why it matters to them.

Most content management platforms will have an area for you to enter the meta description for each page, or you can install a WordPress plugin like **Yoast** that allows you to edit the entire meta description.

To enter a meta description straight into the HTML, the <meta> element will always go inside the <head> element.

It will look similar to:

> <head>
>
> <meta name="description" content="THIS IS YOUR META DESCRIPTION"/>
>
> </head>

NOTE: Every page should have its own unique meta description. Google notices if multiple pages have the same meta description, and many SEO auditing software programs will note redundant meta descriptions as an SEO error.

H1 Tags/Headers/Headings

This element of your page doesn't typically show up in search engine results, but it is the first thing googlers will see after clicking on the page. To make sure they stay there, devote attention to creating effective headlines. Make sure to specify what they'll find there and why they will want to continue reading.

Include some keywords in your headers, pinpoint a benefit your content offers, and give brief hints at what the content covers.

For example:

> "Can't decide which Bible translation to use? Learn the history of the differences between Bible translations"
>
> or
>
> "7 Ways to Simplify Complex Recipes for Easy, Healthy Dinners"

In the example on the next page, "Coping with Depression" is the H1 tag, demonstrating how a keyword should used in the first three words. The subtitle, "Tips for Overcoming Depression..." has specific subtitle formatting, and the subhead "How do you deal with depression" lower on the page is formatted with the H2 tag.

HelpGuide

Your trusted guide to mental health & wellness

Search HelpGuide

MENTAL HEALTH   WELLNESS   RELATIONSHIPS & FAMILY   AGING   ABOUT US

Coping with Depression | H1 tag

When you're depressed, you can't just will yourself to "snap out of it." But these tips can help put you on the road to recovery.

Why is dealing with depression so difficult? | H2 tag

Depression drains your energy, hope, and drive, making it difficult to take the steps that will help you to feel better. Sometimes, just thinking about the things you should do to feel better, like exercising or spending time with friends, can seem exhausting or impossible to put into action.

You designate your text as H1 by adding the <h1> tag to the HTML code, or by selecting "Headline" or "H1" or a similar option from your content management platform in the "Style" section.

This will typically make the text larger and bolded, or possibly a different font, depending on the theme or template you're using.

Each page should have **only *one* H1**.

For subtitles or subheadings, which are excellent for breaking up long text blocks and making the whole post more skimmable, content managers can use H2 or H3 tags, which will typically appear smaller than H1-designated text. H2 and H3 tags do not have an SEO impact, but can enhance readability.

If you can't get into your content management platform at the moment and want to check how a certain paragraph is designated, right click on the page and select "View Page Source" to view the HTML code. You can also highlight the area, right click, and select "Inspect Element" on Macs.

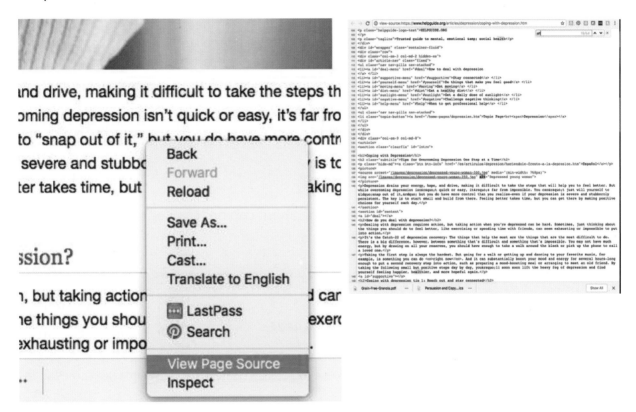

ALT (image) Tags

This code-level text makes images searchable by Google. Also known as an "alt attribute" or "alt description," this HTML tag is applied to an image on your webpage. It doesn't show up on the page, but googlebots pick it up and use it to determine the topic depth of your page.

While Google can determine several aspects about images, Google won't always "see" the message it's intended to illustrate or support. To understand the content of the image, Google relies on ALT tags to determine what the picture is and how well it relates to the topic of the page, which impacts your ranking.

Additionally, ALT tags provide the image information for:

- Visually-impaired googlers using screen readers
- Those who can't see images in their email or browser (if images or HTML is disabled)

When writing your ALT tags, construct a two-to-three-word description of the image and include a relevant keyword. For example, if your page is about sermon tips and you have a picture of a megaphone to illustrate a point, you might use the description, "megaphone; projecting voice for sermons."

Don't make it too long, and make sure not to "keyword stuff" the ALT tag, an old "black-hat[80]" SEO practice that Google will not favor and possibly penalize. For example, for the same image described above on the "sermon tips" page, keyword stuffing might look like: "megaphone sermon tips project voice sermon audience sermon strategies public speaking presentation methods."

Add your ALT text into your content management system, or into the HTML by editing the source code:

<img src="bluemegaphone.jpg" alt="ALT TEXT HERE"/>

For example, in the picture on the previous page about coping with depression, this is how the ALT text appeared in the source code:

```
r-384.jpg 1x, https://www.helpguide.org/wp-content/uploads/sad-woman-blue-sweater-768.jpg 2x" media="(max-w
g" alt="Closeup of sad young woman leaning her elbows against balcony railing, lost in thought"></noscript>
ox=%220%200%20%20%22%3E%3C/svg%3E' data-src="https://www.helpguide.org/wp-content/uploads/sad-woman-blue-sw
```

(Learn more at: **https://moz.com/learn/seo/alt-text**)

Using these seemingly-minor titles and tags can not only improve your SEO but also your user experience, enticing seekers to click on your site as they comb through search results for relevant information.

In summary:

- Your **title tag** answers the "what" questions of seekers. What is this page? What is it about?
- The **meta description** answers "why" they should click on it.
- The **H1 tag** answers a combination of "what," "why," and "how" by introducing the topic and foreshadowing what the content will offer seekers or how it will help them.
- **ALT text** helps Google know that images relate to the subject matter, indicating a more complete page. It also helps visually-impaired people learn what your page is about and what the images are, as they can be read by screen readers.

---

80 Beal, Vangie. "Black Hat SEO (Search Engine Optimization)." *What Is Black Hat SEO? Webopedia Definition*, www.webopedia.com/TERM/B/Black_Hat_SEO.html.

Basic Principles for Creating Strong Social Media Posts

While understanding your audience and developing a content strategy takes a lot of effort, constructing your social media posts is actually pretty straightforward and mostly formulaic. Once you have your content planned out and your target audience determined, there are basic principles to follow to maximize effectiveness across any channel. Even as the technology changes, these principles will largely stay the same. In this section we'll cover how to create posts and write messages for social media that effectively communicate with and engage your target audience.

Main principles for creating a post (also applies to paid ads)

- Get to the point & focus your message.
- Less IS MORE (think snackable content).
- Include a call-to-action (should reflect goals/objectives).
- Include a link (so taking action is easy).
- Limit text in images & use high quality images.
- Video is king.
- Use the lingo of the platform.
- Be honest; no bait-and-switch.
- Include captioning on videos and always provide context.
- Tag relevant accounts. This increases your reach and encourages partners to share.
- Use relevant hashtags.

Visit **SDAdata.org/social-media-resources** for a complete cheat sheet to writing for specific social media platforms.

Guidelines for choosing good visuals (also applies to paid ads)

- Keep it visual; less text is more.
- Optimize your images for each platform.
- High quality (take your own or use stock images).
- Consider the "Rule of Thirds."
- Invoke an emotional response/tell a story.
- People are attracted to bright colors and group shots.
- Keep a consistent look, brand, and color/font palette (see Branding for Ministry).

- Be creative.
- Use contrast to help your image stand out.
- Keep it simple.

It's okay if you don't have a designer on your team to help you create compelling visuals. While proper Photoshop & design training is a valuable asset in communication and should be utilized if at all possible, you are not limited to bad graphics, even if your skillset or resources are limited.

There are a lot of FREE or low-cost web-based tools out there like **Canva** with pre-made templates for social media images. If you're short on high quality images, there are also stock photo resources available online where you can get professional images for free or very low cost.

When laying out your images and designs, utilize the "Rule of Thirds." This guideline divides an image into nine equal parts. Important elements of the image are placed along (or near) intersecting lines. This helps create tension, energy, and increases interest.

Visit **SDAdata.org/branding-image-design-resources** for guidance on free and low-cost stock images, design tips, and branding guides.

General Tips for Getting Your Social Media Posts Noticed

List posts perform well.

This content allows for a highly shareable headline for an article or video: "7 Ways to Reach Young Adults," for example. People love that list posts are highly skimmable and offer clear takeaways. This is what we consider "snackable content." Snackable content is short content that is easily understood, quickly consumed, and memorable.

Use "you" and "your" frequently.

These words tell a person's brain that this message is about them—which draws them in.

Enable your readers to envision a better life.

If readers believe they will learn how to do something better, get an answer to that nagging question, or have their mind blown, they will be more likely to stop and pay attention, as well as share.

Slightly alter headlines for different channels.

By reflecting the culture and expectations of each platform, you're more likely to connect with your audience.

Tug at emotions. Validate people and let them know you're here to help.

Acknowledge your audience's felt needs and tell them how your content addresses their situation. Create conversations, answer questions, solve problems, and address their pain points. Ask questions; even venture assumptions, such as "Feeling stuck?" or "Life is tough." Then offer solutions. Do this without asking for anything in return. Build a relationship based on your service to the community. Refer to **element 3 in the previous section** on writing for online audiences.

Stay real and conversational.

When in doubt, write as though you are writing to a friend. Refer to **element 2 in the previous section** on writing for online audiences.

Example: Feeling defeated? Marriage is hard and you're struggling. We're here for you. Join us for a free seminar. Click here to register in advance and get a free book with 5 practical tips for improving your marriage.

Guidelines for Choosing Hashtags

A hashtag is simply a way for people to search for posts on social media that have a common topic and to join or being a conversation. You may recognize it as the pound sign, or if you're a musician, a sharp sign. Hashtags can be used in many platforms such as Facebook, Twitter, and Instagram. When searching for hashtags on a particular platform, like Twitter, your results will only be pulled from Twitter. To see posts with the same hashtag on other platforms, you must search them separately. Instagram posts with the highest number of engagements have 11 or more hashtags attached.

The ability to create a collective conversation has made hashtags a vital tool for reaching and engaging audiences that share a particular interest. **For maximum impact and reach, use a combination of three types of hashtags:**

Popular. These are widely used or trending hashtags. You can find these in the trending section of Facebook and Twitter or use sites like trendsmap.com. Make sure your hashtags will actually yield results—sometimes people make up hashtags that are never searched, and therefore will not increase your reach. Instead, search for popular hashtags relevant to your post, and use them.

Niche hashtags. These hashtags are less common and tend to reach a targeted audience. For example, to reach the Adventist community you should use hashtags like: #Adventist, #SeventhdayAdventist, #NADadventist, #SDA, #SDAchurch and #HappySabbath.

Branded hashtags. These hashtags should be unique to your brand, not used by anyone else, and should reflect your message in less than 20 characters. Branded hashtags are a great way to reinforce your brand, start a themed conversation, and create a curated stock of content that tells your story. They also enable your audience to engage with you, contribute to the conversation, and become part of a collective story. #DigitalEvangelism and #enditnowNAD are examples of branded hashtag, and you can use them to engage directly with the ministries.

TIP: Hashtags aren't used much on Facebook. The platform's current search capability (as of 2020) isn't polished and, often, relevant posts don't show up when searched. It doesn't necessarily hurt to add a couple hashtags on Facebook to help people understand what you're talking about or reinforce branding. In general, take advantage of hashtags on Instagram and Twitter.

Download the Hashtag library[81] to help with your hashtag strategy.

Anatomy of a Strong Social Media Post

Use the following format to write a practice post for your ministry and brainstorm visuals. Follow this format for each platform the message will be posted to.

Message (Copy):

- Teaser language (1-3 sentences):

_____

_____

_____

----

81 "Adventist Hashtag Library." *Digital Evangelism*, www.sdadata.org/digital-evangelism-blog/adventist-hashtag-library.

- Call-to-action:

  _____

  _____

- Link:

  _____

  _____

- Relevant hashtags (if applicable for the platform):

  _____

  _____

- Relevant accounts to tag (if applicable for the platform):

  _____

  _____

Visual/media: Use the following space to determine if your visual is well suited to your message and goals. (Applicable to either pictures or video.)

- What mood or emotion are you trying to convey?

  _____

  _____

- What mood or emotion are you trying to evoke in your audience?

  _____

  _____

- What story are you trying to tell?

  _____

  _____

- Is the message of the visual focused and clear?

  _____

  _____

- Does your chosen visual tell a story? What is it? Does that story align with your message?

_____

_____

_____

- Does your chosen visual fit in with your overall look and branding?

_____

_____

- Will your visual stand out in the newsfeed, stopping the viewer from scrolling past your message? What can you do to make it stand out?

_____

_____

_____

- Is the visual clear and easy to see on a small screen?

_____

_____

- Is the visual easy to understand without much context?

_____

_____

- Is text on the image or video easy to read on a small screen?

_____

_____

- Does the visual help inspire the viewer to take a specific action?

_____

_____

Examples

https://www.sdadata.org/digital-evangelism-blog/
basic-principles-for-creating-a-strong-social-media-post

Engagers

What's the Role of Engagers?

Engagers are at the front lines of mission and can serve as a powerful mechanism for community care. These empathetic individuals can operate within an organization or independently to engage in online conversations for the purpose of building meaningful relationships, understanding needs, and determining meaningful ways to serve others in both local and online communities.

Every opportunity to connect is an opportunity to advance the kingdom of God. Let's not waste our digital influence. Social media and digital tools provide a unique opportunity for continuous people care that can enhance and strengthen the relationships you cultivate with church members as well as with the community your ministry serves.

Why do we need engagers?

When we consider the roots of the ten leading causes of death (diagram on next page), we can see eight opportunities for the Church body to improve the well-being of others. These eight root causes—stress, a sense of meaningless existence, lack of information/education, anger and frustration, loneliness and social isolation, low self-esteem or self-worth, economic disparity, and helplessness and emotional despair—can be addressed through the corporate Church's messages of hope and wholeness as well as the local church's ability to directly meet the physical and emotional needs of people.

> *"Being listened to is so close to being loved that most people cannot tell the difference."* — *David Oxberg*

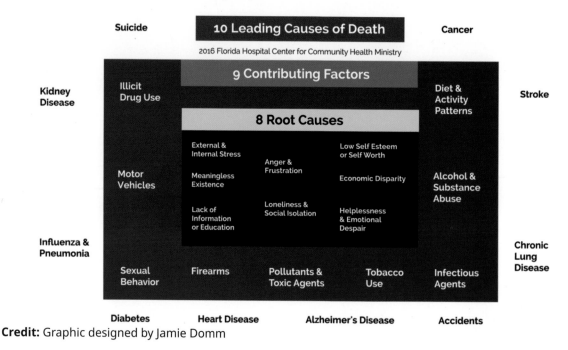

Credit: Graphic designed by Jamie Domm

The Curious Case of Roseto, Pennsylvania

A real-life example of the potential impact of addressing these root causes can be found in the book Outliers by Malcolm Gladwell. He begins the book with the story of an Italian immigrant town in Pennsylvania, whose population was made up entirely of Italians from Roseto, Italy. Due to prejudice, it was common for Italian communities during the early to mid-1900s to develop separately from the general population. The people of Roseto, PA smoked heavily, 41% of their calories came from fat, and many struggled with obesity. Yet they were able to avoid the main causes of death. An extensive study was done of this community, and the secret wasn't diet, exercise, genes, or location. In fact, extended family living elsewhere in the United States did not enjoy the same low rates of disease.

"There was no suicide, no alcoholism, no drug addiction, and very little crime. They didn't have anyone on welfare. Then we looked at peptic ulcers. They didn't have any of those either. These people were dying of old age. That's it."

My mother's family is Sicilian, and I can personally attest to how extraordinary the health of this community was in comparison to that of other Italian-Americans. Italians in the United States tend to eat more meat, more dairy, fewer fresh vegetables, and less fruit than other Americans, and they favor white bread over whole grains; they also tend to suffer from chronic or severe heart issues. This is in sharp contrast to Italians living in Italy, whose health benefits greatly from a more plant-based, Mediterranean diet. However, growing up, we were taught to believe that Italians "just have bad hearts" and that we were genetically predisposed to have strokes and heart attacks. Recently, a man I had grown up with passed away suddenly at age 36. He appeared healthy, but his heart stopped while he was sleeping. Shock rippled through the Italian community followed by knowing nods of acceptance that it's really not that uncommon among us. So, what is the difference between the Roseto community and the community I grew up in?

When the researchers looked beyond the individual and started looking at health in terms of the community, they found something fascinating. Extended family clans formed the foundation of the town's social structure. Three generations lived under one roof, people stopped on the

*"Virtually no one under 55 had died of a heart attack or showed any signs of heart disease... death rate in Roseto was roughly half that of the US...the death rate from all causes... was 30–35% lower than expected."
—Malcolm Gladwell, Outliers*

"...The Rosetans had created a powerful, protective social structure capable of insulating them from the pressures of the modern world. The Rosetans were healthy because of where they were from (paesani culture), because of the world they had created for themselves..." — Malcolm Gladwell, Outliers

street and talked, neighbors took care of neighbors, grandparents were respected, and the people of Roseto were unified through church and civic engagement.

In other words, they avoided illness because they had transported their communal, village way of living—embodied by the paesani culture of Italy—to their new home, whereas the Italian community of my childhood has become disconnected, individualized, and distant, only gathering together at the American Italian Society for major holidays.

To live out our faith and mission in the modern world, we have to be counter-cultural by striving to build healthy communities and support systems. While family and community structures have broken down, the Church, with some effort, can rebuild some of what has been lost to meet the physical, emotional, and spiritual needs of people. While the world has changed, people, fundamentally, have not. We still need each other. Digital tools and technologies offer a way to build meaningful relationships in a busy modern world. This takes empathetic and intentional people who can use their digital influence to uplift and connect with others.

> *"...the values of the world we inhabit and the people we surround ourselves with have a profound effect on who we are."* — *Malcolm Gladwell*

What Does Community in the Digital Space Look Like?

Gorgeous2God is an online ministry dedicated to the difficult issues that teenage girls face. The content is relevant, tackling issues and topics that many don't feel comfortable talking about in church. As of the writing of this guide, the ministry has over 45,000 followers on social media, millions of impressions, and over 200,000 video views. These stats are great, but the real value in something like Gorgeous2God is not the number of likes; it's in meeting a very real need and filling a spiritual void for our teens, who have challenges today that older generations didn't have to face. The advent of the digital age has made navigating young adulthood more complicated, and youth are often left to deal with their problems alone. The need for this ministry is great.

The #gorgeous2god blog has given teen girls a place to search for answers to the challenging questions they face about love, life, health, and faith. I have met so many young girls who are hurting and looking for someone to listen—girls who are suicidal, becoming dependent on alcohol, or who have just shut down completely.

This was the reason we created the Confidential Q & A section of the blog: girls can write in anonymously about anything they are struggling with, and they are answered by a Christian counselor who can show them compassion and offer sound advice without judgment.

—Erica Jones
Assistant Director of Women's Ministries, North American Division

The confidential Q&A part of this ministry serves to create a support system, offering crisis help and community care management. It is the top-visited page on the website, and girls write in from all over on a range of topics, including self-harm, sexuality, loneliness, depression, anxiety, and relationships. When they have nobody they can trust or talk to, Gorgeous2God has given young girls a safe place for Christian guidance on real-life issues. The impact of this ministry is felt through countless testimonials:

"This [person's question] resonated with me on a such a deep level. It's as if this question and response was written just for me. Please keep me in prayer, too, as I struggle with the same temptations."

"This post popped up on my feed at just the right time in my life. It's almost as if you knew my life exactly. Thank you for writing this. Truly, thank you."

What if every church offered a safe place without judgment?

Too often, Christians wall themselves into a protective bubble and don't know how to respond to the difficult realities people face daily. Unfortunately, the feedback that many teens receive feels like it's coming from a position of moral superiority, leaving them feeling judged and isolated.

It's a privilege and a great responsibility when people come to us for answers. It's not just community members either. Church members are not immune to the struggles and temptations of life. Let's give people a safe place to land by demonstrating Jesus' love and compassion for them. The Church should be seen as a place for sinners to find community and help. This is what we should be known for.

Pay attention to cries for help

As a church body, we need to pay attention to cries for help. Every individual has some social influence and can actively use this influence to improve the well-being of others. In a famous example, the actor Pete Davidson from *Saturday Night Live* (SNL) posted online: "I really don't want to be on this Earth anymore." This alarming post resulted in a spur of online messages, phone calls, and people showing up in person to check on him and provide encouragement. Not everyone is famous with millions of followers to analyze their every comment and post, but they are no less valuable to God. The Church body should be setting the example in this kind of community care. It's not uncommon for people to post a cry for help online. If we use our sphere of digital influence to stay connected to our friends and community, we can be there when people need us by simply paying attention and taking action.

> *When we offer a place where people can share without fear of condemnation, where we listen more than we talk, where our advice stems from understanding and compassion rather than moral judgments, they find that the Church—faith—is relevant.*
> — Erica Jones, Assistant Director of Women's Ministries, North American Division

The following are two actual Instagram posts from a friend of mine, who normally shares only her social media best. These tipped me (and others) off that something was very wrong, and we were able to reach out to her in a timely manner to provide the necessary support. Because we had invested time in building a relationship with her in person and online, we recognized this radical departure in posting behavior as a warning sign.

In the mood to delete everything, go missing for a month, get my life back together and come back.

♡ ○ ◁   ⊓

Liked by ████████ and **14 others**
████████ Sums it up. ████████
████████

Be sure to taste your words before you spit them out.

♥ ○ ◁   ⊓

Liked by ████████ and **14 others**

When a church member makes a cry for help online, is the Church body paying attention? We should work to extend the church experience beyond the confines of time and space in a building to an involved community that provides 24/7 support not only to members but also to our broader contacts. We are our brothers' and sisters' keepers. We must really listen and take time in a busy world. We must also go online with purpose, not just for amusement and to pass time. By being intentional, we can make meaningful and measurable differences in people's lives. To be effective, churches should cultivate and nurture healthy communities, both analog and digital, both within the church and in the community, thereby better positioning ourselves to provide a ministry of healing and broad networks of support.

When you invest in building relationships, you can better recognize warning signs and know how to respond.

Recommended action steps:

- Pay attention
- Notice changes in posting behavior and/or language
- Take action/reach out (text, email, call, meet, etc.)
- Ask questions; never assume
- Assess the situation; determine causes and factors
- Listen
- Encourage and uplift
- Pray for and with the person
- Ask them, "what can I do to help?"
- Continue to follow up week after week
- Continue to assess the situation and find ways to help/encourage
- Repeat as long as necessary
- If the person is a victim of a crime, abuse, or other forms of violence, direct them immediately to the proper authorities and resources found here: https://www.enditnownorthamerica.org/get-help
- If a person appears suicidal, direct them to the national suicide prevention center: https://suicidepreventionlifeline.org/

How does community building work in the digital space?

Community building in the digital space works in much the same way as in the physical world. Expert evangelists tell me that the most effective form of evangelism is friendship evangelism. Digital tools simply allow us to scale up friendship evangelism, but this takes getting out of our comfort zone and being intentional about interacting with people, paying attention, and following up in meaningful ways. This kind of outreach can involve every member of the Church, using the communication tools each individual feels the most comfortable with.

Scale up friendship evangelism by:

- Being connected through social media and other digital tools
- Learning more about people's lives through social media in addition to socializing in person
- Taking the time to engage and show interest
- Using digital tools to inform and invite friends to fellowship opportunities/events
- Taking advantage of opportunities to serve people by better understanding their expressed needs, for example, help with moving, distress after loss of a loved one, etc.

- Starting meaningful conversations
- Listening more than you speak
- Utilizing digital tools to follow up and stay in contact with people

Give them Community, Love, and Support

It all starts by connecting with the people you meet inside and outside the Church, understanding that not all online relationships have to remain in the digital space. The closer we get to people, the more involved we can be in their lives, and the more influence we can have. Our goal should be to take them from the digital experience to an in-person experience whenever possible. When we seek daily to serve and uplift others, our faith can have a real-world impact that is relevant to all ages.

According to **The Knot**[82], 19% of brides met their spouse online in 2017, making online dating an increasingly popular way to meet prospective partners. It's natural for us to first connect with people in the digital space before developing more meaningful relationships. The Church shouldn't shy away from this change in culture. Digital discipleship is an opportunity for those gifted in fellowship to build relationships and trust within the local community and beyond.

---

82 Knot, The. "Only 1 in 3 US Marriage Proposals Are a Surprise; Engagement Ring Spend Rises, According to The Knot 2017 Jewelry & Engagement Study." *PR Newswire: Press Release Distribution, Targeting, Monitoring and Marketing*, 26 June 2018, www.prnewswire.com/news-releases/only-1-in-3-us-marriage-proposals-are-a-surprise-engagement-ring-spend-rises-according-to-the-knot-2017-jewelry--engagement-study-300552669.html.

What Does a 360° Community Care Strategy Look Like?

The Proper Care and Feeding of Followers

Social media is a valuable tool for listening to the needs of your audience and building relationships. However, simply having a social media presence is not enough anymore. Your audience expects a response when they engage with you online—often within a few hours.

How your online followers perceive your ministry influences their perception of not only the Adventist Church corporately, but God. Your digital voice may be the only opportunity your followers have to see Christ's love demonstrated in their life.

Strong digital brands create connection and take a comprehensive approach to the member experience. Treat your audience members online as if you're talking with them face-to-face. Their online interactions with you should make them want to experience your faith/mission in person. When they come to you for that personal experience, it should be a continuation of the positive relationship you've built with them online.

Your goal in using social media for ministry ultimately should be to understand and fulfill a need, making a tangible impact in the real world. This means listening and taking action on a daily basis.

Every opportunity to connect is an opportunity to advance the kingdom of God. Do not waste your digital influence. Social media provides a unique opportunity for long-term people care that can enhance and strengthen the relationships you cultivate with members, as well as the community your ministry serves.

People search online for answers to their problems—what better place for the Church to engage them?

If someone approached you in person and told you about a struggle or loss, you would respond, right? But when people pour out their hearts online to you or your ministry, are they getting a timely and meaningful response? Does your church or ministry have a team who is dedicated to responding to people online and providing a network of support? Not everyone is ready to walk through the doors of your church, but we can still show them God's love through the care we provide online.

Your digital content may answer some of their needs or questions, but not all. Be the voice that answers back and engages with them in a meaningful way. This is what we call a 360° community care strategy.

According to the **Sprout Social Index**[83], 90% of surveyed people have used social media in some way to communicate with an organization. What's more, over a third (34.5%) said they preferred social media to traditional channels like phone and email. Like Christ, we should be willing and prepared to meet people where they are, and today, that is frequently online.

360° member/community care includes addressing the negative. By being actively engaged online, you have the opportunity to turn negatives into positives by addressing issues and resolving problems promptly. This is especially relevant to younger generations, who naturally turn to social media first to share their thoughts and feelings. Through a culture of online customer service and digital discipleship, you can build a reputation as an organization that truly cares about its members and the community it serves.

Nearly half (46%) of people have used social media to "call out" or complain about a business. That number jumps even higher when you slice the data by generation. Unsurprisingly, millennials are quick to take their frustration to the keyboard—56% of them have complained or called out brands on social media. **That means that millennials are 43% more likely to call out a brand on social media than other generations (sproutsocial[84]).** Therefore, we should endeavor to be present in the digital spaces where millennials and younger generations are likely to express their dissatisfaction with religion, the Church, or the daily struggles of life. This affords us the opportunity to not only gain a better understanding of the challenges they face but also to intervene in a positive way that can prevent them from leaving the Church or bring them into a community of faith.

We underestimate the power we hold in our online content. Used correctly, social media can help us connect with and mobilize an unbelievable number of people, and the community created there drives real-world changes.
—Kaleb Eisele, Humans of Adventism

Do not underestimate the power of engagement. There's no ROI (return on investment) without it!

Invest the time. Build a committee of digital disciples who are available to respond to comments and messages online promptly, while being human. That means engaging with a personal tone that conveys Christ-like care. It will pay dividends for your mission. By living out our mission online and exemplifying the character of Christ, we can become social media ambassadors for the gospel, who eagerly share our content and messages online.

---

83 Sprout Social. "The Sprout Social Index, Edition VI: Shunning Your Customers on Social?" *Sprout Social*, 7 May 2019, sproutsocial.com/insights/data/q2-2016/.
84 Sprout Social. "The Sprout Social Index, Edition XII: Call-out Culture." *Sprout Social*, 31 May 2019, sproutsocial.com/insights/data/q3-2017/.

Engagement is a Personal Ministry Opportunity.

This is not a job for one person or just for pastors. Too often, pastors are burdened with the responsibility of managing the day-to-day functions of their church while also doing all the work evangelizing to the community. When we leave all the ministering duties to the pastor or elders, we limit the opportunities for church members to grow as disciples. Engagement is a personal ministry opportunity for non-techie, nurturing individuals to be involved in digital discipleship and evangelism on an ongoing basis, from anywhere.

Leaders can divide their teams into three groups based on connections, interests, and talents.

- People dedicated to connecting with church members online and responding to their needs
- People dedicated to responding to comments, questions, and needs directed to the church in the digital space
- Trained digital disciples who intentionally build relationships with non-members online and look for opportunities to serve

Digital interactions should be treated like real-life conversations in which we respond to audience interactions, share community-generated content, and "like" or react to comments. Engagers should follow relevant online conversations and actively participate in a Christ-like manner. Digital disciples should seek to understand their audience's needs and respond in a meaningful way. Building online relationships can impact brand awareness, trust, financial support for ministries, and more. The goal is to break down the perceived barrier between the individual and your corporate brand. Strive to be authentic and as transparent as possible. This is how you build trust and authenticity.

Brands are Communicated, Not Just Created

A brand is based entirely on a person's experience. Think holistically about your engagement strategy, and remember that evangelism is more effective when it is built on a relationship. Therefore, our online identity or Adventist brand and faith must go beyond what we know and the message we have to share; it must be based on how much we care if we are serious about digital evangelism. We must change the way we use social media. Aim to create conversations and meaningful community that bridges the gap between the digital and the real world. Then be prepared to meet in the real world. Remember, brand touchpoints all work together.

There should be no disconnect between how a person is nurtured in the pews and how they are treated online, and vice versa.

Social media is an extension of our church brand and voice online. Our brand is how our church is perceived. As stated previously, our online interactions with people should make them want to experience our faith/mission in person. Then, when they come for that onsite experience, it should be a continuation of the positive relationship you've build with them online. Therefore, your church greeters and hospitality teams are also part of the engagers team. They are the onsite church ambassadors, and the atmosphere they create is vital to the visitor/member experience.

How our online community perceives us influences their perception of not only the Adventist Church corporately but God. Our digital voice may be the only opportunity they have to see Christ's love demonstrated in their life.

The Church should be the clear leader in people care.

Our mission is to maximize the highs; minimize the lows. Loyalty is created when brands help people solve problems and address their felt needs. The Church should be a clear leader in member and visitor experience as well as in people care. Remember that approximately a quarter of people are in crisis at any given moment in North America. We should be using digital tools to understand perceptions and needs to determine the most meaningful ways to serve.

Major corporations know that customer service is the key to long-term growth. Loyalty comes when organizations (brands) help people solve problems and address their felt needs.

Investing time can make a huge difference in the health of the local church and its ability to effectively build relationships with the community it serves. When we use our social influence to listen and ask simple questions like, "Are you okay?" or "How can I help?", the intentionality behind our interactions becomes a powerful witnessing tool. Whether from a personal account or a ministry account, engaging in genuine conversations online is a means to live out Christ's example of meeting people where they are and tending to their needs. We embody the spirit of the good Samaritan every time we respond to a cry for help. A 360° community care strategy is one that is driven by purposely reaching out to whoever we encounter online.

I believe that the next great awakening will be a digital one. We have the ability to preach and live out the gospel in view of millions of people, so let's do it. We need every single one of us to commit to being a digital disciple within our sphere of social influence, using social media and digital tools as vehicles to reach out and care for God's children.

Practical Tips for Digital Discipleship and Engagement

Let the members of your online community know through action that you're fully invested in their lives. This is a Biblical concept found in Romans 12 that can be translated to the modern world.

> Don't just pretend to love others. **Really love them**. Hate what is wrong. Hold tightly to what is good. Love each other with genuine affection, and take delight in honoring each other. Never be lazy, but work hard and serve the Lord enthusiastically. Rejoice in our confident hope. **Be patient in trouble, and keep on praying**. When God's people are in need, be ready to help them. Always be eager to practice hospitality. Bless those who persecute you. Don't curse them; pray that God will bless them.
>
> **Be happy with those who are happy, and weep with those who weep**. Live in harmony with each other. Don't be too proud to enjoy the company of ordinary people. And don't think you know it all! Never pay back evil with more evil. **Do things in such a way that everyone can see you are honorable**. Do all that you can to live in peace with everyone.
> — Romans 12:9–18, NLT

As digital disciples, we can live out Romans 12:15 online. Practically, this means when someone online expresses sadness, anxiety about a life challenge, or excitement about a happy event, we can empathize with them. Engage with their post or send a personal message to let them know you're with them along the way, that you're there if they need help. Be consistent and purposeful in your relationship-building.

As efforts to censor Christian viewpoints online and in the public space intensify, we may be tempted to respond defensively in a way that doesn't represent the character of Christ. However, Jesus calls us to be a practical witness, one that puts Him on display in all aspects of our lives, one that is not easily censored. Jesus sought first to fulfill people's needs; He then invited them to follow. We can use our digital and social influence to gain insights and focus on meeting the mental, physical, and spiritual needs of those around us. Remember, what starts in the digital space can transfer into the real world. Once relationships and trust are built, we can extend our invitation to "taste and see that the Lord is good" (Psalm 34:8, NIV). The gospel of action can further our ministry of hope and wholeness, even when words of truth are silenced or unwelcome.

Our integrity, genuine care for others, honor, and faith in Christ can never be taken from us. Our prayers cannot be blocked from reaching God. Christ's character can never be shut down or banned. By embracing the attitude of a servant first and apologist second, light will shine through us to draw others to the God we represent. Be consistent in building relationships with others who may have very different beliefs. Once they know how much you care, they are more likely to come and reason with you over truth.

Understanding that acceptance does not mean approval, what if we became known as people who listened and helped first—without conditions—and people who proactively seek ways to improve the lives of others in practical, meaningful ways, regardless of who they are and without judgement. What if the Church became a safe place to land regardless of one's affiliation or interest in faith?

People share a surprising amount of information online. It's up to us to act on that information. Modern technology gives us the opportunity to reach into gated communities and closed-off hearts, allowing us to build bridges on common ground. Every post represents a real person, both their experiences and their needs. **What prayers can we answer by simply paying attention?**

The Lord is coming soon because God has made it possible for the gospel to reach the entire world. Digital disciples can change hearts and minds by living out Jesus both online and offline.

Empower People: Small Actions, Big Impact

Most ministries or churches don't need big data; we need the power of the people. Instead of relying on heroes who single-handedly change the world, we need groups of people working together to make the world around us, in our local community, better. To generate real impact, we need to start small, realizing that big changes in a small community can have a ripple effect in the wider world.

Jesus spent time with the community to understand and meet people's needs. This is where digital disciples can play an important role.

Train all the generations in your church to

- Be intentional online with how they spend their time
- Pay attention to the posts of their friends/contacts
- Proactively reach out to friends online or via digital tools
- Take action in appropriate and timely ways

Develop a Relationship-first, Empathy-first Engagement Strategy

This means redefining our notion of success to include metrics outside of attendance and baptisms.

Examples of questions you can ask to gauge success

- How many times did you (or your team) share the love of Christ?
- How many conversations did you start or engage in on social media?
- How are you painting a more authentic picture of yourself, faith, or the church?
- How are you building relationships?
- Do you better understand the needs of those you are connecting with online?
- Have you found meaningful and practical ways to help people?

These questions represent personal ministry opportunities that anyone in the church can pursue through their social influence.

Invest the time to build a team. Build a committee of digital disciples who are available to respond to all online comments and messages to your ministry promptly and in a meaningful way, while being human.

This also means responding to messages in your inbox. Be the voice that answers back quickly when someone reaches out for help. If someone sends your ministry an email or messages your ministry with a prayer request, a challenging question, or a personal crisis, they should not have to wait more than one business day for a response. Even if you can't answer their question right away, it's vital to let them know that you received their message, are praying for them, and will have a response or resources for them shortly.

Christ-like care and an empathy-first engagement checklist:

- ☐ Treat online conversations like real-life conversations
- ☐ Respond in a meaningful way
- ☐ "Like" or react to comments
- ☐ Follow conversations and actively participate
- ☐ Ask questions
- ☐ Seek to understand people and their needs
- ☐ Be authentic and transparent
- ☐ Build trust and strive to break down the perceived barrier between the individual and your "corporate brand" (a.k.a. big Church)

Create Opportunities for Prayer in the Digital Space

Even among the skeptical, there is a longing for someone to care enough to pray for us personally. Social media is a powerful tool for soliciting prayer requests and following up on those requests. Prayer can be just one "like," comment, or message away. Online communication lowers the barrier to asking, making it easy for people to reach out when they can't bring themselves to do it face to face.

I can personally attest to how sending recorded prayers can be a powerful way to minister to others. In the wake of a recent tragedy, I found myself asking, "What if we went beyond 'thoughts and prayers'"? It happens all the time: a friend posts online that they lost a loved one or something else bad happened. We press the "like" button and carefully scroll over to the sad emoji. Then we type below "thoughts and prayers" or something similar.

We're sincere about it, too. The person is in our thoughts, and we are praying for them. But we can take it one step further. **What if they could hear us pray for them?** It impacts people so much more when they hear someone petitioning God on their behalf. In times of crisis, they may not be able to answer the phone, or they may not want to talk to anyone. They can still hear us pray if we send audio recordings of our prayers. This can be done on most smart phones and messaging apps. It's personal and intimate. That extra step that we take to invest in another can have a much more meaningful impact than the standard social media response.

Some additional ideas to use digital tools for prayer include

- Create digital groups for prayer (Facebook, What's App, Slack)
- Host live video sessions weekly to take live prayer requests and pray for people live (YouTube, Instagram, Facebook, etc.)
- Message prayer request contacts weekly to remind people that you're praying for them
- Follow up by sending recorded audio prayers so they can hear you pray for them (or call, FaceTime, etc.)
- Place ads to solicit prayer requests via Facebook messenger
- Create weekly prayer posts and personally respond to every person who requests prayer
- Send prayers and receive requests via Snapchat

> *"I saw that every prayer which is sent up in faith from an honest heart will be heard of God and answered, and the one that sent up the petition will have the blessing when he needs it most, and it will often exceed his expectations. Not a prayer of a true saint is lost if sent up in faith from an honest heart."*
> — *Testimonies for the Church*, volume 1, p. 121

Remember to keep track and follow up regularly. Being intentional will not only impact the lives of those you minister to, but will also strengthen your own belief in prayer as you witness it in action. **You may not get updates from everyone, but be patient and persistent with all your digital discipleship and engagement efforts.**

Additional guidance for assessing your online engagement for ministries

- Check daily for comments, questions, and messages and respond in a timely manner. Not every comment needs to be answered, but you are encouraged to "like" them. Don't forget: engaging with positive comments or messages is an opportunity to affirm and strengthen a relationship. Sometimes, legitimate inquiries or simple misunderstandings are expressed that can open an opportunity to serve the needs of members by providing clarification or rectifying the situation.

- Comments that are offensive should be deleted or hidden immediately, but do not automatically delete negative comments. These are an opportunity to listen and respond to the needs of the community. Depending on the situation, respond publicly to the person or via direct message. Use your discretion. Remove spam posts accordingly.

- Talk with, not at your audience. Follow the conversation and actively participate. Seek to understand their needs, ask questions, and respond in a meaningful way.

- Frame every response with the salvation of others as your number one priority. Be diplomatic, professional, and empathetic. Never respond to a negative comment out of anger, and do not take negative feedback personally. Reflect the values of the Church at all times.

- Redirect people to the proper resources and or departments when needed. Follow up to make sure they received an answer or help with their question.

- If a person seems volatile, do not respond, and hide the comment. If the person is aggressive, block or mute them if needed.

- If the person is a victim of a crime, abuse, or other forms of violence, direct them immediately to the proper authorities and resources found here: **https://www. enditnownorthamerica.org/get-help**

- If a person appears suicidal, direct them to the national suicide prevention center: **https://suicidepreventionlifeline.org/**

- For more guidance on how to respond to comments online regarding your ministry, refer to our **Assessing Your Response Guide for Social Media** on the next page.

Assessing Your Response

You find a blog, video, or social media post about your organization.
How should you respond?

ASSESSMENT
Is it positive?

YES   NO

EVALUATE

CONCURRENCE
Provide a factual and well-cited response that may agree or disagree with the post, using an uplifting tone in either case.

You can affirm the post, let it stand, or provide a positive review.

Do you want to respond?

NO

LET POST STAND
Leave it alone, no response.

"TROLLS"
Is this profile or site dedicated to bashing and degrading others, especially the church, our beliefs, leaders or ministries?

YES — NO

"RAGER"
Is the post a rant, rage, joke, or ridiculing or satirical in nature?

YES — NO

"MISGUIDED"
Are there erroneous facts or other misinformation in the post?

YES — NO

"UNHAPPY MEMBER"
Is the post a result of a negative experience with one of our churches, ministries, leaders, or members?

YES — NO

MONITOR ONLY
Avoid responding to specific posts or individuals as this can sometimes escalate the behavior. Monitor the situation for relevant information, comments, engagements, and potential to go viral. Consider banning repeat offenders/abusers if their activity is harmful to other followers or staff.

FIX THE FACTS
Respond directly with factual information. (Refer to the response considerations below.)

RESTORATION
Rectify the situation, respond, and act upon a reasonable solution. (Refer to the response considerations below.)

RESPOND

SHARE SUCCESS
Proactively share your story and mission with the individual. Thank them for their positive feedback. (Refer to the response considerations below.

FINAL EVALUATION
Base response on present circumstances, the influence of the post, and credibility of the poster.

Will you respond?

NO

LET POST STAND
Leave it alone, no response.

YES   YES   YES

DIGITAL RESPONSE CONSIDERATIONS

TRANSPARENCY
Disclose your church or ministry connection.

SOURCING
Cite your sources by including hyperlinks, video, images, or other references.

TIMELINESS
Take time to craft good responses, but respond within 24 hours as much as possible.

TONE
Respond in a tone that reflects the love of Christ and the standards of the Seventh-day Adventist church

INFLUENCE
Focus your attention on the most influential people and institutions related to your ministry, and the church.

Please remember to reflect the love of Christ always. Though it may be difficult to respond to every post, every opportunity to connect is an opportunity to advance the kingdom. For ministry leaders, understand that social media provides a unique opportunity for long-term pastoral care that can serve to enhance the relationship you cultivate with your members as well as the community your ministry serves.

Social Media + Big Data Services | North American Division | SDAdata.org

Credit: Graphic designed by Brittany McNitt

Sample Guidelines for Hosting Small Groups, Forums or Video Conferences

For those ministries and digital evangelists who decide to host an online small group or Bible discussion, here are sample community guidelines and recommendations to help make it a positive and safe environment for all.

Feel free to adjust to your community's needs. Depending on your audience, you may want to consider a more casual tone.

* * *

We're excited that you have decided to join our online small group/discussion forum. To make this a positive and safe environment for all, please consider the following guidelines and recommendations, which will help us get the most out of our shared experience.

Guidelines

Confidentiality What's said in group discussions, stays in the group. This is the most important ground rule. No one wants to find out that he or she has been the subject of gossip or well-meaning "prayer discussions." Always ask permission before sharing personal or sensitive information about another person. Do not publish, post, or release information that is considered confidential. This includes private medical information without direct approval from the person or their family. Follow federal requirements such as the *Health Insurance Portability and Accountability Act* (HIPAA) of 1996 and the *Family Educational Rights and Privacy Act* (FERPA).

Be honest and transparent Please maintain integrity and honesty to help foster trust in the relationships we develop within our online group.

Timing To be respectful of those with tight schedules, we ask that participants join live chats or video conferences on time. You are a big part of making this an interesting and fulfilling group!

Participation Everyone should commit to participate both as a listener and as a speaker.

Preparedness Please do your best to complete readings and research ahead of time so you can get the most out of our discussion sessions and also feel empowered to contribute.

Minimize distractions When utilizing video conferences, as much as possible, please limit background noise and distractions, turn off or silence your mobile device, refrain from taking phone calls during discussions, and put your microphone on "mute" if you're not speaking.

Be respectful and remember your manners We recognize and value diversity of opinion within our online community. Therefore, we ask that you please always seek empathy first, and do not interrupt when others are speaking. Be tolerant towards others' viewpoints; respectfully disagree when opinions do not align. We encourage comments that are reasonable and related to the topic being discussed as long as they are presented in a manner that is constructive, polite, and respectful, honoring the dignity of others in the process. Avoid putdowns of any kind. Treat others online as you would treat them in real life. Be encouraging of one another. Everyone is in a different place spiritually; do your best to be understanding and supportive.

Tone of voice We want to welcome all into our community and create a place for open and honest discussion. Let's make sure our tone of voice is friendly, positive, welcoming, and uplifting, as though we are speaking to each other in person. This is especially important in comments or text, as lack of speech inflection and body language can make the meaning seem harsher than what was intended. Avoid condescending language. Strive to be open, empathetic, and engaging. Let's be a community that is committed to encouraging people with different experiences and perspectives to share their ideas in a productive manner, building a bridge of empathy, understanding, and respect. We are all at different places in our spiritual journey; let's strive to be supportive.

Posting frequency We would love for everyone to commit to posting regularly, but we understand that some may feel more comfortable just following the conversation, especially in the beginning. For those who want to contribute directly to the discussions, remember that quality of content is more important than quantity. Stay engaged in the conversation, but don't post too much and overwhelm or take over the conversation. We all want to be and should be heard. Let's commit to respecting others' perspectives and desire to share. It's important to listen more than we speak and to create space for everyone to contribute.

Share your story Be human, have fun, exchange ideas, and connect with others. Let's allow our lives to act as powerful witnesses of God at work as well as an encouragement to others. Humbly sharing our walk of faith, our doubts, and the challenges we face involves a great deal of vulnerability. This vulnerability can be our strength as we remove the masks we all wear and create a community of support through real connections based on authenticity, shared values, and goals.

Content We encourage comments that are reasonably related to the topic being discussed, as long as they are presented in a manner that is constructive. Refrain from posting advertisements, political statements, sales promotions, or spam. Do not share inaccurate, irrelevant, or misleading information that is off-topic or self-serving. This means that your multi-level marketing posts will need to find another home.

Protect yourself and loved ones Be careful about what personal information you share online, and regularly check your privacy settings. Never publicly share your home address, social security numbers, login credentials to ANY account (especially passwords), credit card information, security question answers, or complete birth date, etc.

Act responsibly and ethically Be honest, be professional, and be kind. Always verify questionable content with credible sources before sharing information, and remember to honor others' privacy. Respect the intellectual property rights of others, and always give credit where credit is due.

Images and language Do not post sexually explicit images of yourself or others. Do not use insulting, demeaning, vulgar, prejudiced, racist, threatening, or violent language or profanities. Avoid gossip, mean-spirited comments, mocking or shaming others, bullying, making false statements against others, and any other behavior that causes emotional harm or distress. Members who attack other members will be removed from the group to maintain a safe environment.

Avoid conflict Avoid publicly discussing controversial topics such as politics where emotions can run high and result in inflammatory or inappropriate discussions. Take it offline, have a private discussion, or simply do not respond. Always show respect for others' opinions. When dealing with complex or emotional issues is necessary, frame responses in a positive way that seeks to bridge the divide. God loves all His children, and His children are a diverse people.

Consequences

Appropriate action will be taken when these guidelines are violated. A warning may be given but is not guaranteed; in severe cases, violations can mean removal from the group. Community members should voice concerns and report behavior that violates the guidelines to the administrator via private message. The administrator reserves the right to remove inappropriate comments or content without notice.

Agreement

By joining this community, you are considered to be in agreement with the terms and conditions listed above.

As the mediator/leader for this online group, I commit to:

- Following the conversation and actively participating; checking daily for comments, questions, and messages, and responding in a timely and meaningful way; seeking to understand and meet the expressed needs of the community.

- Deleting any spam posts and offensive comments immediately; taking constructive feedback seriously as an opportunity to listen to and respond to the needs of our community.

- Removing advertisements, political statements, and sales promotions immediately.

- Making sure that our community is uplifting and safe; therefore, any member who attacks or bullies another member will be removed from the group.

- Reflecting our community values at all times and framing every response with the spiritual and emotional health of members as a priority; being diplomatic, professional, and empathetic.

- Redirecting members to proper resources when needed or desired; always following up to make sure members received an answer or help with their question.

Digital
Disciples and
Missionaries

Growing as Digital Disciples

Content creation, engagement, and distribution are not limited to the official church brand and accounts. Make it a point to reach out to young people and let them know that their talents in this area are highly valued even if they are not part of the core team. Some people just need permission and a little mentorship to realize their talents and passion for personal ministry. Everyone has social influence through texting, messenger applications, email, and social media. Encourage and inspire them to use it to build God's kingdom.

The two primary roles in which digital disciples can serve are as engagers and distributors. For this reason, I have decided to unpack the role of digital disciples here in the guide, in-between these two sections of the digital discipleship and evangelism model.

The Bible tells us to become and make disciples. God calls us all to serve in unique ways. Ellen White encourages us to:

> *"Let every worker in the Master's vineyard, study, plan, devise methods, to reach the people where they are. We must do something out of the common course of things. We must arrest the attention. We must be deadly in earnest. We are on the very verge of times of trouble and perplexities that are scarcely dreamed of."*
> *– Ellen White, Letter 20, 1893*

Identify people in your church who can be digital disciples, all on their own, as a means to further the mission of your church. This allows and empowers members to engage in ministry and discipleship in ways that aligns with their passion, spiritual gifts, tools of preference, and personal style. There is a spiritual void online because we are not doing enough individually as members or collectively as a Church. The mission field is wide open, it's our duty to share the gospel through the tools available to us.

The Great Commission given to us by Jesus Christ states, "Go, therefore, and make disciples of **all the nations**" (Matthew 28:19). An easy and free way to reach the nations lies in the palms of our hands. When we hesitate to make the gospel message more available, we allow our own human weaknesses and fears to get in the way of our mission. How can we justify this resistance to boldly declaring our faith online? We live in an era of religious freedom with minimal persecution in North America (in contrast to what is happening in other parts of the world). However, the predominant perception among the Church body is that evangelism is an event run exclusively by a specific set of people.

In Exodus 4:2, God asks Moses "What is in your hand?" and tells him to lead the children of Israel to the promised land. To Moses, his staff is simply a tool for directing sheep, but with God's direction, it becomes an instrument through which miracles are performed. If God spoke to each of us today, we would answer, "a phone," a "laptop," or an "iPad." Most of us have a smart phone that can be used either for distraction or for positive impact. The responsibility of every disciple is to utilize every available resource for God so at the end of the age, when we face our Master, we will hear, "Well done, good and faithful servant!..." (Matthew 25:23). We must commit to work diligently online to share present truth, regardless of who we are and what our official role may be in the Church.

Tips and Ideas for Individual Digital Disciples

- Share your faith through daily digital activities (texting, Instagram, group chats, Snapchat, Facebook posts, blogging, etc.).

- Invite your online community to join you in learning more about knowing, loving, and serving God.

- Be willing to humbly share the story of your life as a Christian. For example, share how you've felt God's presence even when you've made poor choices. Honestly tell how you deal with specific challenges with God's help. Explain what guides your choices. Describe the joy and comfort loving God gives you in today's troubled world.

- Pay attention to what your friends share with you directly and online. Listen with care. Follow up and see how they are doing. Respond to requests for help. Rejoice over their personal victories. Offer to pray with and for them. Record audio prayers and send them to the person throughout the week. Keep track of prayer requests, check back with the person for updates, offer ongoing encouragement, and celebrate God at work in their life. Assess and respond to their expressed needs. Remember, God has called us to serve without judgment.

- Go out of your way to include and uplift friends and followers who are shunned, ignored, or bullied online.

- Support your church's ministries with personal resources (time, talent, and finances). Offer to help with online content creation, updating the website, or funding a community outreach social media ad.

- Reflect the character of Christ in all your digital and in-person interactions with others. Being a disciple involves all of your life, including your life lived online.

- Pray for guidance to detect where God is calling you to serve. Support those with digital callings.

- Evaluate the culture of the platform through which you feel called to serve to more effectively reach people within your sphere of influence.

Adapted from growingfruitfuldisciples.com

Digital Discipleship Commitments

Grow God's kingdom by:

- Building networks for friendship, fellowship, and support through your digital influence

- Looking for physical, mental, social, and spiritual needs within your community

- Responding mercifully to the discovered needs in a relevant way

- Acting compassionately on behalf of people who are disadvantaged or at risk
- Praying for the Holy Spirit to prepare you to reach others for Christ
- Using your social influence to help tell the world the story of Jesus
- Being able to give a reason for your faith when asked
- Using your social influence to share the story of your personal relationship with Jesus
- Being willing to be humble and honest when sharing your personal spiritual journey

By living out our mission online and exemplifying the character of Christ, we can become social media ambassadors for the gospel, impacting not only our local communities, but the world.

Balancing Digital Mission Work and Spiritual Health

Inspired by Dee Casper, Director, CORE at Pennsylvania Conference of Seventh-day Adventists

For digital missionaries who spend significant time online working to further the gospel, it's important that we learn to safeguard our own spirituality as well as develop a healthy work-life balance. Another way to frame this is to make sure you are fed spiritually before you minister to others.

> *"Then, because so many people were coming and going that they did not even have a chance to eat, he said to them, 'Come with me by yourselves to a quiet place and get some rest.' So they went away by themselves in a boat to a solitary place." — Mark 6:31–32 NIV*

This can be a huge challenge because when you work for a religious organization, EVERYTHING seems important because of the eternal impact of the work. And there seems to be no end to the work that needs to be done. Those of us who have chosen this type of career are self-driven but also driven by the expectations (or perceived expectations) of others. How do we prioritize? How do we set boundaries that enable us to get the job done, while taking care of our own spiritual health?

We're not in this alone. God knows our limitations, and He doesn't want us to work so hard that we work ourselves away from Him—the relationship that matters the most. This is why He has given us the Holy Spirit. After we've given it our all for the day and go home to rest, the Holy Spirit keeps working.

He also doesn't want us to dive so deep into the mission field that we become corrupted by it. There are a lot of toxic conversations and content on social media, just as physical mission fields have their dangers and temptations. If the early missionaries of our Church had stayed away from the mission field because of the dangers, the Seventh-day Adventist Church would never have become a global movement. We must go where the people are and minister to their needs, while simultaneously guarding the avenues of our own heart.

Here are four tips for digital missionaries to help balance digital media and spiritual health.

1. **Guard the edges of your day**. Start and end the day without social media. I can easily become consumed by social media; it's my job at least eight hours a day. If I don't set healthy boundaries for myself, the negative aspects of social media start to drag me down and prevent me from really resting. Rest can take many forms, but I cannot rest by spending hours on personal social media when I work all day on those same platforms. What many consider pleasure just feels like more work. When I'm

not working, I consume media and information the old-fashioned way by reading magazines and books, etc. Also, in the morning, I make it a point to follow Jesus' example and begin with solitary prayer and Bible study...with a physical Bible.

"Very early in the morning, while it was still dark, Jesus got up, left the house, and went off to a solitary place, where he prayed." – Mark 1:35 NIV

The peace of the morning enables me to think clearly and connect with God. I know that the moment work begins, I will be connected on multiple platforms for at least eight hours, so this "analog" devotional time is sacred. When the day is done, I disconnect and again turn to print material, exercise, and face-to-face conversations to help me wind down. Staying connected online throughout the evening can **disrupt your sleep and result in depression**[85]. If you browse social media to stave off loneliness and pain, you will find the exact opposite of what you're looking for.

2. **Structure your digital evangelism/discipleship and personal life like a missionary outpost center**. A physical outpost center is a place outside the city where you can get away from your daily work and connect with God. It's a missionary community that provides education, restoration, and preparation for work to be done in the city, where missionaries will return to win people's trust and friendship with the intention of winning souls for Christ. Social media is a similar means of building bridges and relationships with people to create a positive influence within the community. Use the connective power of social media to share your faith and show your friends that you care about them. Social media is a center of influence for discipleship and friend evangelism. But remember to maintain your outpost center, a distinctly separate part of your life where you can recalibrate and then go back to your mission field stronger than ever. Don't live in social media, and don't let your world be controlled by it.

"When duty calls us to this, we should be doubly watchful and prayerful, that, through the grace of Christ we may stand uncorrupted." – Ellen G. White, *Messages to Young People* 419.1

3. **Digital missionaries must have a clear purpose for getting on social media.** My friend Dee Casper (Director, CORE at Pennsylvania Conference of Seventh-day Adventists) asks us to treat social media like a post office. Typically, at a post office, you enter, pick up mail, and drop off outgoing mail and packages. Most people don't hang out all day in a post office. That would be strange. If we go online with a plan, this helps prevent us from getting distracted from our original purpose and mission. Go on social media to drop off some content, pick up some content, connect with your friends, check performance stats, and then leave. Don't move in. We've all had the experience where we intend to watch one video, and two hours later, we don't know how the time got away—never accomplishing what we actually set out to do.

---

85 Breus, Michael J. "Tweeting, Not Sleeping? Balancing Sleep and Social Media." *Psychology Today*, Sussex Publishers, 28 Jan. 2016, www.psychologytoday.com/us/blog/sleep-newzzz/201601/tweeting-not-sleeping-balancing-sleep-and-social-media.

4. **When you're lonely and have nothing to do, don't try to fill the void by going online**. It's like going grocery shopping when you're hungry. Temptation will always take you further than you want to go when you're vulnerable. Social media is a tool; don't let it use you. Go there to serve, not be served.

   "We may be placed in trying positions, for many cannot have their surroundings what they would; but we should not voluntarily expose ourselves to influences that are unfavorable to the formation of Christian character." – Ellen G. White, *Messages to Young People* **419.1**

God has not called us to live in social media but to influence people through social media. Our influence online can stretch much further than we imagine with the help of the Holy Spirit.

God has called us to use our digital influence for Him, whether we have an audience of four or 40,000. We plant the seeds; God grows the seeds. People pour out their hearts online. We can be there in their moments of crisis with love, hope, and truth. But in order for them to listen to us, we must carefully cultivate and use our digital influence purposefully.

By setting boundaries and sticking with them, we can be better equipped to help others.

We're All Publishers Now; Responsible Use of Your Social Media Influence

He who is careless and heedless in uttering words or in writing words for publication to be sent broadcast into the world, sending forth expressions that can never be taken back, is disqualifying himself to be entrusted with the sacred work that devolves upon Christ's followers at this time.
— Ellen G. White, Counsels to Writers and Editors

Long before audio-visual equipment was invented, Ellen White knew how to do the figurative mic drop better than anyone.

This quote is a powerful and relevant reminder of the solemn task we have been charged with. I encourage everyone who is on social media, especially digital missionaries, to read her **Counsels to Writers and Editors**.

Social media has eased entry into the world of telling stories, sharing ideas, and expressing thoughts to a wide audience. It used to be that if you wanted to tell your story to a broad audience, you had to buy your way in through costly traditional media. Times have changed; we are all writers and publishers now. But with this ability comes responsibility.

> *Social media is the ultimate equalizer. It gives a voice and a platform to anyone willing to engage.*
> *— Amy Jo Martin*

Social media, in its essence, is people connecting with people to create a collective human story. We all want to be heard, and we all now have a platform for public speaking. You can have hundreds, thousands, even millions of people viewing your messages. But, as so often is the case, the person we need to set boundaries with is ourselves.

Your personal social media is a great opportunity to share your story and contribute to the collective conversation. It can serve as a powerful witnessing tool, revealing what God is accomplishing through you and your work. But...

Would someone know you are a Christian based on your social media? What values are you reflecting? Would your audience like Christians based on your behavior online?

I once listened to a powerful sermon in which the speaker asked, "If you were pulled into court today, is there enough evidence in your life to convict you of being a Christian?" Well, what evidence does your social media provide? Is your use of social media driving people away from the Church or toward Christ? Think about it.

Social media is public by nature and has blurred the lines between your work for the Church and your personal life. This can be a good thing. Follow principles of responsible use and be a living testimony to others. Be a light among the quagmire of negativity online.

Every opportunity to share is an opportunity to either advance or hinder the kingdom of God. People should use social media; it is a powerful tool. After all, the appeal of social media is that it reflects a basic human need, and that need is to connect and share. As digital disciples, that means connecting with each other and God as well as sharing the gospel.

Let your light shine before men in such a way that they may see your good works, and glorify your Father who is in heaven.
— *Matthew 5:16*

It is likely that you have friends or followers on social media who are not Christians or who are questioning and struggling with their faith. As a member of the Church, you are always representing the Church even if you are not actively engaged in digital evangelism. This is especially true for pastors and others in leaderships roles. It is of vital importance that we maintain a high standard of ethics, striving to always be honest, professional, and kind. This means always verifying questionable content with credible sources before sharing, honoring the privacy of others, respecting intellectual property rights, and never releasing confidential information. However, you may share official statements from Church leadership.

Your posts can have a much greater impact and reach than you imagine. We recognize and value diversity of opinion within our community, but as an employee or member, your followers may confuse your opinion with the official position of the Church. While this is most likely not your intention, be mindful to:

- Prevent confusion by avoiding posts that conflict with your ministry's official positions on matters

- Observe principles of impartiality

- Avoid topics like politics where emotions can run high and can result in inflammatory or inappropriate language

Many discussions are significantly more productive in person. It is generally accepted that 93% of our communication is non-verbal (Mehrabian & Wiener, 1967; Mehrabian & Ferris, 1967). Online communication strips away the context of tone and intention. Many comments online are misunderstood without this context and provoke controversy and conflict instead of positive discourse. When asked why they left the Church, a sizable portion of former members cite something that was said to them or how they were treated by other members. My question to you is this:

How many people are you willing to drive out of the Church to make a point or to "win" your argument?

Public figures have the potential to magnify division and take thousands out of the Church. As individuals, we may discourage someone from even considering Christianity. We talk about a life lived as a reflection of Christ but turn into devils on social media. People say things online that they would never dare to say in person, and then wonder why their ministry efforts are not bearing fruit. We were all taught in primary school to T.H.I.N.K. before we speak. It is not enough for something to be **True**; it must also be **Helpful, Inspiring, Necessary**, and **Kind**. This is especially true in online communication.

Because of the power social media can have, it's crucial that we consider the effects our content will have on our audience. Both our negativity and our positivity grow exponentially as they are spread by our audience and friends online. When it comes to church, we can create a community of people that attack or a community of people that heal.
— Kaleb Eisele, Humans of Adventism

We absolutely respect and value different perspectives among our members and ministry leaders. But as representatives of the Church, we must not use our public speaking platforms as a sounding board for the problems we see in the Church, in leadership, and in our country. We are a family; let's resolve our internal issues privately. It would be considered obscene to go knocking on doors and to begin your evangelistic effort by lambasting the very Church you are asking people to join. So why do it online? We must protect our Church family and frame all of our digital communications with the salvation of others in mind. Social media is a powerful tool for sharing the gospel; let's use it wisely and err on the side of caution.

The power and efficiency of our work depend largely on the character of the literature [message] that comes from our presses [social media profiles]. Therefore, great care should be exercised in the choice and preparation of the matter that is to go to the world. The greatest caution and discrimination are needed. Our energies should be devoted to the publication of literature [posts] of the purest quality and the most elevating character. Our periodicals [blogs, videos, and updates] must go forth laden with truth that has a vital, spiritual interest for the people.
— Ellen G. White, Counsels to Writers and Editors

Freedom of speech does not mean freedom from consequences. Carelessness in speech can and will inhibit our ability to accomplish our mission. When we turn people away from the Church, we are not only working against ourselves, we are working against God. You can also get your ministry or self in legal trouble. If you work for the Church, you may endanger your job and reputation. This can be avoided by using discretion and focusing on the positive, such as what God is accomplishing through your church or ministry. Let's

> *Finally, brothers, whatever is true, whatever is noble, whatever is right, whatever is lovely, whatever is admirable— if anything is excellent or praiseworthy, think about such things. — Philippians 4:8*

not fall into the trap of using the negative and sensational to get attention online when God calls us to focus on what is good and holy.

We all have the same goal. I truly believe that social media is a vital tool for accomplishing our mission in the 21st century. Young people are leaving the Church at a startling rate. They spend up to 18 hours a day behind a screen, and nine hours of that time is spent on social media. What messages are you sending them? We must take the gospel where they are, and not where we want them to be. But when our actions and our speech contradict each other, we only have ourselves to blame for the rising egression. Let's work together to get the job done and go home.

And this gospel of the kingdom will be preached in all the world as a witness to all the nations, and then the end will come. — Matthew 24:14

Personal Social Media Audit: Questions to Ask Yourself

A checklist for cleaning up your digital influence to avoid embarrassing situations and misunderstandings

If you're reading this guide, you're probably a church/ministry employee or digital missionary with a potentially large digital influence. What you do with that influence matters. We've all made mistakes communicating online, but it's never too late to start fresh by conducting a personal social media audit. Below is a checklist to help you evaluate your social media profiles and identify areas for potential change or improvement. Whether you have four friends or 4,000, as disciples, we must strive to reflect Christ always, drawing others to His life-saving truths and love. We cannot do this effectively when our words or actions send mixed or divisive messages.

Social media is public by nature and has blurred the lines between a person's ministry life and personal life. No matter how high your privacy settings are, your activity is always public at some level. As representatives of a faith group, your individual accounts are no longer just personal. This can be a positive thing. Each of us is called to be a disciple, and this includes reaching the digital mission field. I believe that God is calling a generation of youth to the digital mission field but, to be effective, we must begin by setting healthy boundaries with ourselves.

I encourage you to read through these questions carefully and make any necessary changes to your social media profiles. This may include removing old posts and pictures. In some cases, deleting accounts may be necessary.

Personal social media audit checklist

❏ **Do you list your employer or ministry on your social media profiles?**

Brand your posts as personal and your own opinion. Employees are generally allowed to associate themselves with their organization, but they should clearly brand their posts as personal views and purely their own opinions.

❏ **Are you sharing your faith with personal stories?**

Share your story. Be human, have fun, exchange ideas, and connect with others. Your life and work can be a powerful witness of what God is accomplishing through you.

❏ **Are you taking the necessary precautions to protect your and your loved ones' personal information?**

Protect yourself and loved ones. Be careful about what personal information you share online, and regularly check your privacy settings. Never publicly share your home address, social security numbers, login credentials to ANY account (especially passwords), credit card information, security question answers, or complete birth date. Only "friend" people who you actually know.

❏ **Are you spreading "inflammatory speculations," "rumors and gossip," or confidential information?**

Act responsibly and ethically. Be honest, be professional, and be kind. Always verify questionable content with credible sources before sharing information, and remember to honor others' privacy. Do not publish, post, or release information that is considered confidential. Remember, you can be held personally liable for content you publish online. Follow federal privacy requirements as described in the **Health Insurance Portability and Accountability Act**[86] (HIPAA) of 1996 and the **Family Educational Rights and Privacy Act**[87] (FERPA). Make corrections to mistakes quickly and apologize.

❏ **Are you giving credit where credit is due?**

Respect the intellectual property rights of others. It's okay to share; just don't claim the work or the words of others as your own.

❏ **Would people know that you are a Christian based on your social media? Would they like Christians based on your social media?**

Represent your faith values. Social media can be a powerful witnessing tool. Remember that your posts can have a greater impact and reach than you realize. Diversity of opinion is respected and valued within the Church community, but as a ministry leader, your followers may confuse your opinion with the official position of the Church. While this is most likely not your intention, prevent confusion by avoiding posts that conflict with your organization's official positions and observe principles of impartiality.

Follow the golden rule. Do to others as you would have them do to you: Luke 6:31. This means avoiding gossip, mean-spirited comments, mocking or shaming others, bullying, and any other behavior that causes emotional harm or distress.

❏ **Do you have any content on your profiles that would be potentially embarrassing if an employer, grandparent, or respected mentor saw it?**

Use only uplifting images and language. Do not post sexually explicit images of yourself or others. Do not use profanities or violent language.

---

86 HHS Office of the Secretary,Office for Civil Rights, and Ocr. "Summary of the HIPAA Privacy Rule." *HHS.gov*, US Department of Health and Human Services, 26 July 2013, www.hhs.gov/hipaa/for-professionals/privacy/laws-regulations/index.html.
87 "Family Educational Rights and Privacy Act (FERPA)." *Home*, US Department of Education (ED), 1 Mar. 2018, www2.ed.gov/policy/gen/guid/fpco/ferpa/index.html.

❏ **Do you find yourself in heated discussions online? Do you ever write comments online that you would never say to a person's face?**

> **Avoid conflict**. Avoid publicly discussing controversial topics where emotions can run high and can result in inflammatory or inappropriate discussions. Take it offline, have a private discussion, or simply do not respond. Always show respect for others' opinions. As members and leaders in the Seventh-day Adventist Church, we represent a diverse people with a diverse set of ideas, experiences, and perspectives. We cannot properly serve when we are dismissive of certain groups and ideas.

> **A special note regarding politics:** The North American Division does not officially endorse any candidate or political party. Voting choices are strictly up to the individual. Church leaders and employees should not inadvertently or intentionally use their influence to advocate for their political preferences. Employees of the Church should maintain principles of impartially and avoid promoting their political viewpoints on any of their social media profiles. Let us reflect Christ and His love at all times—and avoid public political discussions and conflict. We also recommend that independent digital missionaries also follow this principle.

❏ **Do you air your work frustrations online or gossip about co-workers?**

> **Protect your work family**. Everyone has good and bad days. Do not air work grievances on social media or use your channels as a sounding board for the problems you see in the Church. Others may be negatively impacted and turn away from the Church. You could also embarrass yourself or endanger your job. The Adventist community is very closely connected online, so your posts may be widely seen. It is always best to seek counsel offline and/or direct your concerns to HR. Focus on the positive and, like any family, resolve issues privately.

❏ **Have your opinions, habits, faith, or attitudes changed over the years?**

> **Remove old posts or accounts that may reflect poorly on you or no longer represent your beliefs**. Old posts or accounts that misrepresent who we are now may detract from our ability to be effective witnesses, especially as many people seek to find fault with us. We are all growing in our faith and developing our character. It's a good idea to clean up old posts or profiles that are no longer relevant to who we are now.

❏ **Do you find yourself glued to your phone, losing track of time, and not accomplishing what you need to do? Do you browse social media until bedtime and then have difficulty getting to sleep?**

> **Create balance**. Social media can be addictive; know when to turn it off. It is healthy to take breaks from social media. Don't let social media affect your job performance or your personal life. Tune out roughly two hours before bedtime for optimal sleep, don't check social media while driving or walking, and maintain good posture. Refer to the section on balancing digital media and spiritual health.

In summary, if you are unsure whether or not to share or write something online, err on the safe side and don't post it. It's likely that you have friends who are not Christians or who may be struggling with their faith. Don't be another reason for them to leave their church. Find ways to use your digital influence to encourage others and share your faith in positive ways.

If you are forgetful about or ignore the guidelines above, a few things could happen.

You could:

- Inhibit the ability of the Church to accomplish its mission
- Turn someone away from the Church
- Get your organization into legal trouble
- Get fired

A special note to employers and supervisors

In regard to a Church employee sharing their personal life on their social media profiles, "offences" must be evaluated on whether the content or behavior is in clear violation of Church doctrine, and it is not to be gauged by individual preferences or interpretation.

> *And the times of this ignorance God winked at; but now commandeth all men everywhere to repent.*
> *— Acts 17:30*

Behavior on social media prior to conversion or a re-commitment to the faith should not be used against an employee who is now a member of the Church in good standing.

On a personal note, I converted in my early 20s from atheism. I have since lived as a committed Adventist for over 13 years. Until I did a personal social media audit, if you dug far enough back in my post history, you'd find images of me drinking wine and eating unclean meats because this is what many non-Adventist Italians are culturally raised to do. At the time, I did not know that there was a Biblical way of living healthier. This was prior to my conversion and my commitment to the health principles, and I think it's important that we understand that personal social media often captures snapshots at different points of an individual's spiritual journey. Given the gospel of grace, these snapshots should not be held against a person years after conversion and seasons of dedicated service. By removing old content that does not reflect who we have become, we can prevent it from sending mixed messages to those we witness to online or providing fuel to those who seek to find fault.

Distributors

What is the Role of Distributors?

This might be heretical to ask, but are we too focused on church attendance, at least in the short term? I cannot help but wonder if the 2020 COVID-19 pandemic crisis is a wake-up call to the Church. Churches have been forced to shut their doors to help reduce the spread of the virus. Knowing what the Bible warns about end-time events, this is not going to be a unique historical moment but rather just a precursor to the time of trouble. The Church will need to rely more and more on digital technologies. The time to develop the necessary skills and shift our understanding of what church means is now. Remember, church is not a building, it's a people. When fleeing persecution, the early Church took the gospel to new regions out of necessity. So, too, we must now take the gospel message to the digital mission field and spread our message of hope and wholeness when it is needed most.

> *Modern technologies have decentralized the gospel message.*

It used to be that people would have to travel, sometimes long distances, to hear the gospel message from a preacher or evangelist. Now, we can browse speakers on YouTube from the comfort of our home. Until recently, the barrier to entry was so high in publishing that only the top theologians, pastors, and authors could get their writings into the public's hands. With the advent of social media, blogs, and vlogs, we're all publishers now, and we can each be distribution centers within our areas of digital influence.

We don't have a message problem

We have the gospel—the greatest story ever told—of Christ's birth, life, self-sacrificing death, resurrection, and soon return. As the Seventh-day Adventist Church, we also have the Three Angels' Messages, sent to all of God's children in every nation, tribe, tongue, and people. We, as a people, have the gift of prophecy, the guidance of Ellen G. White, and a health message for better living.

> *We don't have a message problem; we have a distribution problem.*

The role of distributors in the Digital Discipleship and Evangelism model is to use digital tools and technologies to share these messages within their sphere of digital influence.

Although we're facing the biggest communication shift in 500 years, church communication hasn't really changed in thirty years. I can't help but wonder if God is using COVID-19 to push the Church into the digital age. While God doesn't cause suffering, He can—just as when the early Church fled persecution and spread the gospel—use the pandemic to accomplish His will. Hopefully, in a few years time, we'll look back and recognize this crisis as the catalyst that resulted in a major communication shift for the Church.

"And we know that God causes all things to work together for good to those who love God, to those who are called according to His purpose (Romans 8:28, NASB)."

Five hundred years ago, the Gutenberg press* was developed, and it revolutionized the world and helped rapidly spread the gospel. It dramatically sped up the process and reduced the cost of printing. It altered society through the unrestricted circulation of information and the increase in literacy. The printing of the Gutenberg Bible marked the start of the so-called "Gutenberg Revolution" and played a key role in the Protestant Reformation. Just as the Protestant reformers leveraged the printing press, we must use digital tools to share our message. Again, society and the way we communicate has been dramatically altered. It has never been easier to communicate, but it's also never been harder to cut through the noise. Therefore, it is essential to be intentional and strategic with how we use digital tools to spread our message.

*Note: It's only fair to mention that several Asian civilizations had developed a type of printing technology prior to the Gutenberg press. These cultures did not adopt it as rapidly nor as widely as Europe did. Therefore, these earlier versions did not impact civilization to the same extent as the European technology.

Digital as a distribution tool

I firmly believe the next great awakening will be a digital one. It will take each and every one of us acting as digital disciples to share the gospel and spread the Three Angels' Messages, with a loud voice, to the ends of the earth. We can start by reaching those within our own spheres of digital influence. We use digital tools every day to communicate and share ideas, yet we have not leveraged their potential for kingdom building. We are all called to be disciples, to be distributors of the gospel. To share truth through these powerful technologies—this is our generation's Great Commission.

The mission field is next door, and it's just as legitimate.

Faith is on the decline in Western society. Put simply, we have become the mission field. Instead of hopping on a plane to reach people where they are, we can now go online and use the platforms people use to share hope and wholeness in a way that is accessible and comfortable for them.

But to reach the world, we must first reach our neighbors.

Challenge question: How well do you really know your neighbors and your community? It's never been easier to connect, but as a society we've become disconnected from our immediate community. Why is it so hard to connect with and reach people?

People are busy. We're overworked, overloaded, and overwhelmed, trying to keep up with a constantly growing to-do list. Many people are just trying to get by and get through the day. How many of us feel this way? Why would we expect our target audiences to be any different? Perhaps we lack community because we do not have time or energy left for our neighbors. This, of course, is the Devil's design; keep people busy enough that they don't have time for each other or for God.

> *The mass of men lead lives of quiet desperation.*
> *—Henry David Thoreau*

Amid the chaos, the younger generations feel safe behind their screens, which provide a degree of distance and anonymity. Remember, on average across all age groups, we spend almost **three times as much time socializing on social media as we do socializing in person**[88]. This dramatically increases for individuals under 30 years old. Remember, if you want to reach people, you must go where they are and spend time with them. As I've said in previous sections, today, that means going online to share our messages.

---

88 Asano, Evan. "How Much Time Do People Spend on Social Media? [Infographic]." *Social Media Today*, 4 Jan. 2017, www.socialmediatoday.com/marketing/how-much-time-do-people-spend-social-media-infographic.

How to Engage in Digital Door-Knocking

It's hard to knock on someone's door, even if we already know them. In fact, it's not even socially acceptable nowadays to just show up unexpectedly at someone's house in case they are busy when we stop by. We must call and schedule a visit first. Add the need for social (physical) distancing, and it becomes clear that the old way of evangelizing can no longer be the primary method. But you don't have to knock on a stranger's door to share your faith. Nor do you have to create the content. Canvassers are not also the authors of the books they sell. The burden of content creation is not for all of us.

Social media allows us to share our faith and engage with our community when it's most convenient for them. It allows our audience to self-select whether or not they want to engage.

Young people spend upwards of 9 to 18+ hours behind a screen each day. That's a lot of opportunity for us to share and reach people anywhere. Excluding periods of sleep and quarantine, how many people are normally home nine hours a day to answer the door? In normal daily life, many people leave the house early and come home late at night.

Digital door-knocking is when you share spiritual content on your social media profiles or through messaging and email to create an opportunity for people to engage with you about your faith. The spiritual content can be anything (a picture, text, video, blog, etc.); just be sure to include with it a personalized message about how it impacted you. Your friends and followers can scroll past it or choose to engage when it's convenient for them. Given that a lot of people could be stuck at home with extra time on their hands because of COVID-19 or a future crisis, social media may be their main source of entertainment and connection. There's a lot of opportunity right now for us to share and reach people everywhere using digital technologies. Success can no longer be measured only by counting people in a building but, rather, we must consider whether or not we're building a kingdom.

World-of-mouth opportunities online

Word-of-mouth is still the strongest marketing mechanism for getting the word out about a product or cause. People always trust the opinion of their friends and family over what a brand says about itself. This is why reviews and testimonies are so powerful. We participate in word-of-mouth marketing every time we share about a product or experience with others. We might share in person, but word-of-mouth marketing often takes place on social media and through messaging applications and texting, etc. We do this constantly when it comes to our other interests and don't even realize it. In terms of sharing the gospel, this just means doing the thing you do all the time online but doing it for the kingdom. In other words, be intentional with what you share.

Here are some digital ways individuals can distribute our messages

- Forward emails.
- Text invitations with an info link to contacts, or send invitations via messenger apps.
- Share content from your church's profiles or a ministry you follow and add a personalized message.
- Live-stream events, sermons, Bible study groups, etc., from your social media profiles.
- Hit "like," "love," or "wow" on ministry Facebook posts to increase organic reach.
- Post to community groups or apps like Next Door about upcoming events.
- Find digital ways to connect with neighbors and community; then share your faith with them.
- Follow, friend, or join online Christian groups to help increase their digital influence.

Leverage social influence through pods

Create a culture of sharing and content engagement within your church community. Nearly everyone is on social media. Even if you have an older congregation, a good many of them are likely on Facebook and have an email address. Don't assume that they are not; ask and find out what platforms they use.

Social influence can be both analog and digital. Churches do well with analog distribution (printed flyers for example); however, we need to start leveraging the digital social influence of our members. Even in a small church with 50 congregants, if half were on social media and were connected to just 50 people within the community (outside of the congregation), that's a potential reach of 1,250 people. This is a low estimate, but you get the idea. Train your membership to function like a social media "pod." A "pod" is a group used to increase engagement on social media platforms like Instagram and Facebook but can apply even to email. Members of a pod agree to comment, like, and share each other's content or the content of a particular entity such as a church or ministry. Teach your membership to engage and share your church content on a weekly basis as a form of evangelism/outreach.

Pod commitments vary but typically fall into three categories

1. All users must engage with every post within an hour.
2. All users must engage with every post within 24 hours.
3. All users must engage with relevant posts whenever they can.

A congregation that understands the value of participating in ministry this way could serve as a powerful reach vehicle for souls. To realize this potential, they must be equipped and encouraged. Determine members' strengths and train them to use their strengths.

Be sure to

- Take time in meetings and during service or choir rehearsals to prioritize technology.
- Provide hands-on training to church members.
- Ask them to take out their phones and take action right in the moment.
- Empower a designated person to post about key events to local groups or community apps like Next Door.
- Encourage members to mark Facebook events with "going" or "interested" to increase organic reach.
- Encourage them to invite others to events via email/text or on Facebook.
- Encourage them to "like," "wow," or "love" important content on your Facebook profile (and other social media platforms); this increases organic traffic.
- Tell them when to expect emails and ask them to forward emails to their contacts.
- Send out weekly emails with links to content you want members to share or engage with.
- Keep them posted on how their efforts are working and create a sense of teamwork.
- Get them excited about digital discipleship through sharing your excitement and testimonies about how it has worked.

Holiday test case

My local church is predominantly older, and we have around 200 members—not a mega church by any standard. For our holiday programs and special events, the leadership asks me to lead promotion. Beyond targeting the community with social advertising, I also spend a lot of time rallying the membership to hand out flyers, forward emails, share on social media, text people, etc. This is new for them and out of their comfort zone, but we are a close-knit community, and our members really do seek to help each other.

At the end of our six-week campaign for our annual Christmas play, 393 tickets had been reserved in advance, and on the day of the event, we packed the house with around 500 in attendance. Now, the DC-Metropolitan area has a lot of holiday opportunities, so people did not have to choose us. By and large, most people who reserved tickets online said they had heard about the event from a friend or family member, via email or social media. Word-of-mouth out-performed paid social advertising. For our previous event at Easter, by contrast, with no promotion strategy and much less competition in the area, only 100 tickets were reserved in advance.

After the Christmas play, we sent a survey follow-up to gather feedback to better understand our audience and let them know that we valued their opinion. This allowed us to understand how many non-Adventists attended the program. In this case, 20% of survey respondents were not Adventists. It also gave us an opportunity for service by adding this question: Is there anything we can help you with? Let us know how we can bless you, and please provide your contact information.

Here is an example of how with the right coaching, even an older congregation can realize their untapped potential for helping their church better reach the local community through increased awareness. This example served as a test run and, since then, all the tickets for our special programs have been reserved in advance of the event.

This example had immediate results, but having a congregation that consistently engages in digital door-knocking would have a long-tail effect that we may not fully appreciate this side of heaven. Using this model, our messages of hope and wholeness could be spread to every corner of the digital space and, while not everyone is able to walk through the door of a church, they will be able to connect with God.

Magnifying Your Reach through Partnerships

"No person will make a great business who wants to do it all himself or get all the credit."
—Andrew Carnegie

Active social media partnerships are key to expanding your reach and branding. Social media is designed for community building, so create and cultivate online relationships with other ministries and organizations. Find organizations to build partnerships with either by location or topic. It is likely that you already have partnerships in place for creating events. Magnify their value by partnering for your digital communications campaign for the event. Be sure to make sure your partnerships are mutually beneficial to both parties. Don't ask for any favors that you're not willing to grant yourself. People will figure out quickly if it's a one-sided relationship, and you'll end up closing the door to future collaborations.

Who can you work with?

- Sponsors/donors
- Organizations and ministries already involved in the event
- Participants/speakers
- Local churches/related organizations
- Conferences and unions

Most of time, events don't happen in a silo but rather involve several partners. I have found time and time again that active social media partnerships are a key element in successfully promoting events on social media. If you reach out to 10 contacts who each have a "small" social media following of 1,000 people, your message suddenly has the potential to reach up to 10,000 people online. Reach out to more contacts, with bigger fan bases, and you can see how your reach can grow exponentially.

Communicators typically have a lot on their plates, and social media manager may be just one of many hats that they wear throughout the work week. Contacts are often willing to promote partner events through their various digital channels, but time and resources are limited. With this reality in mind, providing your partners with a "promotions packet" is an effective and easy way to equip your contacts with the resources they need to easily become social media ambassadors and share your message.

Normally, when marketers reach out to contacts to ask for promotion on their behalf, there is an assumption that the partner will write the posts and generate the content. As a result, most requests are not prioritized and do not realize their full potential. A promotions packet, on the other hand, provides recommendations, pre-made social media posts, eNewsletter blurbs, tracking links, graphics, branded hashtags, and more. The social media manager needs only to copy and paste from the Word document and schedule. They can of course modify the message for their audience if desired or necessary, but they don't have the burden of generating content. This approach also has the added benefit of allowing you to control the quality and consistency of your brand's message as it is distributed through your partner's channels.

I encourage you to create your own promotions packets following best practices for creating social media posts and to develop digital partnerships to help expand your reach in future campaigns. In a world of limited budgets, this approach costs you only time and effort.

One last important note: Make sure that when you reach out for help with promoting your ministry, you are not only willing to reciprocate but also able to follow through with such agreements. Partnerships should be mutually beneficial, and trust can be built and cultivated over time when both parties follow through on their promises.

Social Media Advertising for Churches & Ministries

Most local churches and ministries have limited budgets. To make the most of your limited ad dollars, build your advertising on top of your organic distribution mechanism. Paid ads are most successful when they are accompanied by strong digital distribution. They enable you to reach further than you can organically and to target specific groups of people for outreach efforts.

Why spend any money when you can use the platforms for free?

Social media platforms are businesses that need to make money; therefore, they limit unpaid reach. This means less than 5–10% of your fan base (depending on the platform) will naturally receive your posts in their news feed. You can counteract this by promoting key posts to reach more of your fan base and by placing ads to expand your reach to new audiences.

To get started:

- Determine your target audiences (who you want to reach). Refer back to the section on understanding your audience for guidance.

- Determine your budget (how much you can spend).

- Start with a test, and then expand based on results.

How much is appropriate to spend?

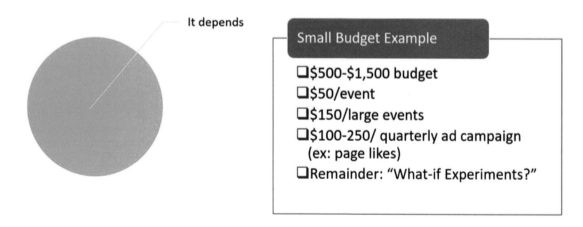

It depends

Small Budget Example

- ☐ $500-$1,500 budget
- ☐ $50/event
- ☐ $150/large events
- ☐ $100-250/ quarterly ad campaign (ex: page likes)
- ☐ Remainder: "What-if Experiments?"

Credit: Graphic designed by Jamie Domm

A lot of people ask me, "How much does it cost to promote an event online?" But the beauty of social media ads is that the answer depends on what you can afford. Social media works very well for small budgets and non-profits. A little can go a long way, but it's important to spend some money. As your confidence grows, and your familiarity with reaching your target audiences grows, you can increase your budget as needed. Ultimately, your budget depends on the size of your goals and your purpose. A small, local ministry may need to spend only $300 a year, whereas a nationwide campaign would need to spend at least $3,000 to create impact within a targeted audience. For all organizations, I recommend starting with a small ad budget and a clear objective that is easy to measure. This way you can learn and maximize your results as you grow.

How can a small church or ministry fund their ad budget?

Look for monies that can be redirected. Businesses that must balance their budgets or make a profit put most of their effort behind what is working. We should be just as shrewd. Too often, we pool our best resources and people into efforts with limited potential out of a misguided attempt to be fair or to meet accepted expectations.

This will be different for every church or ministry, but it's time to take a critical look at our programs. Determine your church's strengths, and put all your efforts behind them. The **Strength Finder**[89] (now CliftonStrengths) program operates on this premise for individuals and teams. We all love underdog or David and Goliath stories, where individuals or organizations overcome their weaknesses and beat the odds, but for most, thriving comes when we embrace what we are naturally good at. The underdog stories are typically outliers, and we should not operate under the assumption that we, too, are the exception to the rule. First, improve the functions required for your church's operations, and put money behind keystone ministries with the most potential in the context of your membership and community. It might seem unfair to those ministries that don't get as much support, but like the parable of the talents, you need to invest in the areas that are working the most effectively. Good stewardship means focusing on places where you can make an impact beyond day-to-day operations.

Do not place a single ad until you have a clear understanding of what you are trying to achieve and whom you are trying to reach.

Another option is to find individuals willing to fund social advertising as an outreach initiative or personal ministry. I personally fund and run my local church's social media advertising and website hosting. Over time, our church leadership has learned the value and potential of using these digital technologies for a variety of purposes.

Who should take responsibility for managing social advertising?

Not every church is blessed with an experienced digital strategist, but this is an opportunity to allow a member with knowledge or interest in digital communications or marketing to develop their skills in a personal ministry that aligns with their abilities. If your church has staff, your communications lead can manage your ad account. This could

---

89 Gallup, Inc. "StrengthsFinder 2.0." *Gallup.com*, Gallup, 30 Jan. 2020, www.gallup.com/cliftonstrengths/en/strengthsfinder.aspx.

also be a valuable skill for a younger member of your pastoral team to learn and take responsibility for. Either way, be sure to provide oversight so that expectations are clear, and the budget is respected.

Types of ads

As of 2020, Facebook still has the most sophisticated social media advertising platform for small organizations. It enables detailed targeting for small budgets on Facebook, Instagram, and third-party websites. However, many of these ad types are also relevant to other platforms. The technologies and platforms may change, but these "types" will still be relevant, regardless of the platform. Choose the types of ads that align with the key performance indicators discussed in the strong foundation section of this guide.

Here are the main types of ads that can be placed

- **Promote your page/profile.** Increase page "likes" and awareness within a targeted community
- **Website ads.** Increase traffic to your website for a specific event/offer/ information from members of a particular community
- **Posts targeted to members and those who follow or engage with your page.** Improve internal communication
- **Ads targeted to your subscriber email list.** Improve internal communication/ awareness
- **Video views to targeted audiences.** Increase impact/expand the reach of your message
- **Event response ads.** Increase event/program awareness and attendance
- **Messenger ads.** Help facilitate conversation or generate leads for Bible studies
- **Lead generation ads.** Offer free materials and collect outreach lead contact information
- **Retargeted messages.** Based on behaviors such as content engagement and website visits that enable advertisers to follow up with relevant messages

Basic targeting for social ads: Reaching the right people without breaking the bank

Refer back to the section on understanding your audience, and use this framework to determine who your audience is and how you are going to target them through social advertising. Targeting allows you to maximize your ad dollars by ensuring you reach the right people instead of wasting money on those less likely to respond.

Most platforms allow you to target by:

- **Location** (e.g., country, state, city, address, or place)
- **Age**
- **Gender**
- **Language**
- **Interest:** Choose multiple to reach people interested in a specific topic or who are part of a particular group
- **Connection:** Fans of your page and their friends (or email list)
- **Behavior:** People who have interacted with specific content on your website

Optimize the effectiveness of your ads by:

- Limiting text in images and using high quality images
- Providing context but keeping text brief
- Targeting your ads to stretch your advertising dollars
- Including a clear call-to-action
- Being honest—no bait-and-switch marketing
- Including closed captions on videos
- Promoting content or programs that align with the felt needs of your target audience
- Familiarizing yourself with ad terminology and monitoring your campaigns closely
- Using trackable links in ads that direct traffic to your website to monitor performance in Google Analytics
- Setting up **Google Analytics**[90] on your ministry's website so you can monitor and understand how visitors interact with your website and where they come from

Always follow the basic principles for writing a strong social media post, discussed previously in this guide.

Make ads personal

The right message is one that resonates with a felt need. When it comes to messaging and programming, make sure you are addressing a pain point or felt need within your target audience. Strive to understand those in your community, and tailor your outreach efforts and messaging accordingly. Remember, show empathy first, validate their experiences, be genuine, and offer practical advice/solutions/resources.

Never assume you know what your audience is interested in. Do the research, and create content and opportunities that meet people where they are in their spiritual journey. You can have the best targeting and the most well-crafted posts, but if the "product" is tone deaf to the real needs of the community you're trying to reach, your ads will fail.

_____

90 "*Google*, Google, analytics.google.com/analytics/web/provision/#/provision.

When crafting your message, follow this formula

Empathy + Caring + Authentic + Practical Advice/Resources/Solutions

Example message: Marriage is hard; we're here to help. Join us for a free marriage program where you'll learn practical tips for improving your marriage.

Beware of vanity metrics

When placing ads, make sure you're strategizing for impact. Many of us can get caught up in vanity metrics such as how many followers we have. Remember, it's not about how many people are following you online. The real question is, are people growing closer to Jesus because of your digital strategy? Perhaps your video received only 200 views, but if 200 people showed up for a Bible study, most of us would be ecstatic. Every view, comment, share, download, etc. represents a real person who has been influenced by your content and messages.

An Introduction to Facebook Pixels with Custom Audiences

What is a Facebook pixel? What are some of its practical uses for ministry?

Simply put, a Facebook pixel is a small snippet of HTML code that is placed on your website for tracking purposes. It's similar to Google Analytics but specifically for Facebook, enabling advertisers to target and re-target more effectively. Installing a pixel allows Facebook to track visitors and categorize them in custom audience groups. This information can help you develop more effective ads that appeal to a specific audience's interests while saving money.

It takes time, effort, and money to attract an audience, so once you have people actively engaging with your content, the next most effective step you can take for your ministry is to cultivate your relationship with your audience. Pixels are one way to re-engage your followers/visitors and ensure that your content is reaching them. Pixels can also help you customize the content they receive, taking into consideration their level of engagement and behavior and making sure your organization's content stays relevant to their needs.

For example, suppose you have a website that tackles multiple difficult topics, and one of the most visited areas focuses on "What happens when we die?" You can re-target visitors to that specific page with Facebook ads for videos, new content, free books, etc., all related to a biblical perspective on death. You can do the same for your prophecy, health, and Sabbath sections as well.

Custom audience options for pixels include:

- All web visitors
- People who visited specific pages
- Visitors by time spent
- Visitors by date

Another practical ministry example: Let's say you are promoting a series of content highlighting health principles; you're getting a lot of traffic and engagement on your website, but only a few people are taking advantage of the free book offer. A Facebook pixel allows you to re-target these engaged website visitors with a Facebook ad reminder to download or request the free book. This increases your conversion rate (offer downloads) by focusing on people who have already showed interest but who may have gotten distracted by the demands of work, family, and life. Modern life means people are busy. They may be indeed be interested but may need reminders (remember the "Rule of 7"). This is particularly true when it comes to advertisements for events.

Facebook Business offers a **step-by-step guide**[91] on how to set up a Facebook pixel for tracking.

Key custom and saved audiences for churches

Once you have your pixel set up, you'll also want to set up custom audiences in your ad account so you can strategically target certain types of people who are more likely to respond to your content and invitations. Once these are set up, Facebook will dynamically build up these audiences for your use in targeting ad campaigns. These audiences are considered warm audiences because of their relationship to your page and are generally more cost efficient. You can also create lookalike audiences and colder or broader audiences for wider outreach efforts.

Keep these saved in your Facebook Ads manager for easy access when setting up campaigns.

Facebook page engagers in the past 90, 180, or 365 days. People who have already expressed interest in your church and/or content

Video engagement audiences. For example, you can re-target those who watch church service livestreams or video messages

Website visitors in the past 90, 180, or 365 days. People familiar with you who have taken some interest

People who have visited specific website pages. For example, Bible studies, youth pages, visitor pages, etc.

Lookalike audience of page engagers. This is an easy way to find the top 1% of people similar to those already engaged; this audience is automatically formed at the national level, so you will need to geo-target by address when using this audience

Lookalike audience of email list. People similar to people who have subscribed to your eNewsletters

Lookalike audiences of those who signed up for events, reserved tickets, downloaded free books, etc., via online forms. People similar to those who have attended previous programs or received materials

Parents with children in the age ranges relevant to your programs. Such as VBS and Pathfinders who live within driving distance

Saved audience by age and/or gender geo-targeted to your community. Ideal for men/women's ministries, teen/young adult ministries, etc.

---

91 "Create and Install a Facebook Pixel." *Facebook Business Help Center*, www.facebook.com/business/help/952192354843755?id=1205376682832142.

Everyone within five miles of your church. If you are located in a rural area, the distance can be increased, or the distance can be reduced for more densely populated areas. Aim for an audience of less than 50,000 people for cold ads inviting people to marriage programs, holiday events, etc.

To learn more about Facebook advertising, visit facebook.com/business

The Basics of
Data Tracking & Analytics

If you can track it, you can measure it. As a result, you can gain a better understanding of your audience and their behavior, helping you adapt your strategies to more effectively reach them. Taking the time to review the performance of your digital communications and platforms enables you to better understand what is working and what needs to be changed, which empowers you to shape your digital communications strategy based on data. In the long run, this will save both time and money while maximizing impact.

Avoid data paralysis

Time is valuable. Don't get so caught up in the details of the data that you respond too late and miss an opportunity. Aim to stay ahead of the curve and be proactive instead of reactive in your strategies.

Most ministries and churches do not have the luxury of a dedicated analytics team, but you don't need to dive too deep to get valuable information about how your website and campaigns are performing. Since most ministries are new to digital communications and analytics, we're going to stick to a high-level overview. Go back to those key performance indicators we discussed in the strong foundations section, and use those as a guide for what to track based on your ministry's goals.

Take the time to familiarize yourself with the terminology of the various data points. Most analytics tools define their terms within the platform. You can usually access these definitions by hovering your cursor over the question mark next to the data category.

The data that is most important to your efforts will be:

- Website performance data
- Social media platform analytics or insights
- Social advertising performance reports

Compare the information you find to the performance goals and metrics you established. Always look for areas of improvement and adjust accordingly.

Communicate with everyone involved by:

- Sharing report summaries with your team (both good and bad)
- Creating summary reports for management, committees or boards; keep detailed reports for yourself
- Problem-solving as a team; sometimes the best solutions are found outside your industry/department/specialty

Use trackable links (a.k.a. UTM codes)

UTM codes are segments appended to a URL that enable data platforms like Google Analytics to record information about website visitors and traffic sources. This is vital for social media managers as it enables you to measure and prove social media success or, alternatively, identify problems and adjust your strategies. Creating trackable links is surprisingly easy to do and will give you valuable insights into how well your digital communications and ads are performing.

What is a UTM code?

UTM = **Urchin Tracking Module**

Example: https://www.SDAdata.org/?&utm_campaign=DigitalGuide-2020&utm_source=Social-Media

UTM codes can be used in links shared via:

- Social media posts
- Email
- Online ads
- Websites
- Any link that drives traffic to your website

Creating your own trackable links

A trackable link has five building blocks:

1. The URL you want to direct people to
2. A ? to signify the start of the UTM code
3. & + UTM
4. The name of the promotional campaign the link is related to
5. The source where the link will be used

Example:

URL – https://www.sdadata.org/digital-discipleship-and-evangelism.html

Campaign – DigitalGuide-2020

Source – Social-Media

Put it all together using this formula

Regular link + ?&UTM + Campaign (what event, month, where, etc.) + &UTM + Source (channel/platform)

Final result:

https://www.sdadata.org/digital-discipleship-and-evangelism.
html?&utm_campaign=DigitalGuide-2020&utm_source=Social-Media

Be sure to always test your links!

After you create your trackable link, be sure to test it to make sure it works. It can be very frustrating for your audience to receive digital content with a broken link.

Website performance data

The most common analytics tool for detailed website performance tracking is **Google Analytics**[92]. Google Analytics is a free tool for monitoring where your visitors come from and understanding how they interact with your website. It's easy to **set up a free Google Analytics account**[93]. Most website hosting platforms offer easy-to-follow directions to get you started. Once you are set up, take the time to familiarize yourself with the tool and make it a habit to check your website's analytics each month.

Terms and definitions

Session. A visit to the website during which the user is active

Users. Number of unique people who have visited your website during a specific time frame

Page views. Total number of pages viewed; repeated views of a page by a single user are counted

Page/session. Average number of pages viewed during a session

Average session duration. Average length of a session

Bounce rate. The percentage of single-page sessions in which there was no interaction with the page

Key metrics to monitor

Demographics: Age and gender. Known data about your website visitors.

Geo: Location. You can see location by country, city, state, and metro area. You can also look at language if that is relevant to your ministry.

---

92 *"Google,* Google, analytics.google.com/analytics/web/provision/#/provision.
93 "How to Set up Google Analytics." *Digital Evangelism*, www.sdadata.org/digital-evangelism-blog/how-to-set-up-google-analytics.

Behavior: Site content – page. Here, you can determine your most popular and least popular pages.

Behavior: Engagement. Length of visit/depth of visit.

Acquisition and traffic sources. As communicators, we want to know what is working and what is not working to drive people to our website.

The channel (or traffic sources) breakdown

- Other = UTM codes or campaigns
- Direct (visitors typed in the URL)
- Social media (no tracking code)
- Referral from another website
- Search engine (e.g., Google, Bing, etc.)
- Paid search (results from Google Ads)

Campaign performance

When you drill down deeper under campaigns, you can learn what aspects of a campaign performed the best by using unique UTM campaign names for the different components of your communications strategy. Google Analytics automatically picks up the campaign name and source from the tracking links. There is no need to do anything in Google Analytics to make this work! Just be consistent with the UTM codes you use, and be clear with your campaign and source names.

Remember, **prioritize**. You don't have time to track everything, nor do you need to!

Once you have determined what you're going to track to determine whether or not you're reaching your goals, check performance monthly, and record your results in a way that enables you to see trends over time. Some analytics tools like Google Analytics allow you to create dashboards for easy access, while social media insights may require that you create your own charts and graphs. To learn more about Google Analytics, check out our **beginner tutorial on SDAdata.org**[94].

Social media analytics or insights

Most social media platforms offer at least basic insights into the performance of a ministry's account and who their audience is. Take the time to familiarize yourself with the analytics for your social media platforms and regularly check them to understand trends over time.

---

94 "Beginner Tutorial for Google Analytics." *Digital Evangelism*, www.sdadata.org/digital-evangelism-blog/beginner-tutorial-for-google-analytics.

Pay particular attention to:

Demographics. Who follows/likes your page by location, age, gender, and language.

Engagement. This includes comments, likes, shares, messages, video views, etc. If you're creating content that resonates with your audience, you should expect to see strong engagement rates.

Video views. A more reliable metric for gauging success than number of views is how many minutes are spent watching your videos and the number of thru plays. Many platforms count a few seconds of watch time as a view, so the number of views can be misleading.

Peak visit/engagement periods. Knowing when your profile traffic peaks and when your audience is most likely to engage with your content will enable you to schedule your content strategically.

Social advertising performance analytics

After you place your ads, don't wait until the campaign is over to check performance. Monitor the ads closely to make changes and optimize as needed. Catch problems early on; otherwise, your money may go to waste. The great thing about social advertising is that you can edit campaigns at any time if they are not meeting your expectations. Make sure you understand what the numbers mean; most platforms have descriptions available in pop-ups next to the column head.

Be sure to:

- Understand where your ads are appearing and what locations have the strongest results.
- Determine who you are reaching by age, gender and location. You may find that your ad doesn't resonate with who you thought it would or that your targeting was off.
- Monitor engagement/response. Are you getting the results you expected?
- Test images, messages, and audiences (A/B testing) to learn what type of ad and messaging performs the best with your target audience.
- Connect performance to Google Analytics and monitor visitor behavior using trackable links.

Some basic terminology you should know:

- **Results.** The number of times your ad achieved an outcome, based on the objective you selected
- **Reach.** The number of people who saw your ads at least once; reach is different from impressions, which may include multiple views of your ads by the same people
- **Impressions.** The number of times your ads were viewed

- **Frequency.** The average number of times each person saw your ad
- **Cost per result.** The average cost per result from your ads
- **Cost per impression.** The average cost per impression of your ads
- **Relevance.** An estimation of how well your target audience is responding to your ad
- **Click-through rate (CTR).** The percentage of times people performed a click after viewing your ad
- **Cost per thousand (CPM).** The average cost per 1,000 impressions
- **Cost per click (CPC).** The average cost for each click

Track so that you can learn

Remember, if you're going to take the time to put together a campaign strategy, take the time to track its performance so you can be better informed next time. There's no point in testing strategies without tracking your efforts. If you don't learn from your campaign, you can't improve the next one. Social media and digital marketing are both an art and a science. Use data to inform your intuition.

Part 3
What's
Next?

The Change We Need:
What the New Church Should Look Like

You might be tempted to think that we will return to normal in a few weeks or a few months. We will return to normal, but it will be a new normal.
— Chuck Scroggins, Executive Director at the Center for Church Communication

In the weeks after COVID-19 shut down churches across America and the world, I saw an unprecedented amount of creativity and innovation from churches and ministry leaders. What was previously considered impossible or unimportant became both possible and important overnight. For many, such as the physically disabled and those unable to attend church in person for other reasons, these changes were welcome and long-anticipated accommodations—accommodations that should have been offered when the technology first became available. Our hesitancy to embrace change left many behind and isolated long before COVID-19. It's unfortunate that it took a pandemic to motivate the Church to embrace digital technologies.

Change is not only possible but also necessary. Now, we must figure out together what the "new Church" should look like. When the dust final settles, society will return to a new normal with new habits and expectations. The changes we make (or don't) will set us up for success or failure in the years to come. As always, the Lord is our Rock in troubled times; let's be sure to petition Him daily for wisdom, strength, and guidance as we press forward.

First and foremost, online church must be different. It can't be just a streamed program of people in a building. Church is not a program or a building; it's a faith community sharing a relationship with God and taking action to improve the well-being of others. We must consider the experience of the individuals participating and think empathically about what they expect and need. We must consider how to best serve and involve both those attending in person (when permitted) and online.

Beyond meeting the spiritual needs of church members, digital technologies can be used to mobilize a congregation for community and service in the digital space. What starts in the digital space is not necessarily, nor ultimately, confined to the digital space. These tools and technologies can create impact in the real world and be leveraged to meet the real physical needs of the community. We can continue to be the hands of Christ reaching out to help others in their need; it may just be in a way that is different from what we're currently comfortable with.

We must think creatively about how the "church experience" can be translated to the digital space. This will take the creativity and innovation of everyone, experimenting and trying new things to figure out what works best. It will be different for each congregation and community. We are now in a period of rapid development, innovation, and customization. It's an exciting time, and I am personally energized seeing God working through His Church during this time of change.

This also means that our choice of our "home" church is no longer restricted by physical location. Churches that adapt well will draw members from everywhere to their online church experience. The barriers to entry that once prevented people from attending in person have been stripped away. During the COVID-19 lockdown, those who were previously at a disadvantage found themselves on equal footing with the rest of the community. When COVID-19 is all over, the structures we are now implementing should stay in place to continue to reach those we've previously left behind. Besides, we know the scriptures: this may be only the beginning of such troubles. There will be more pestilence and an ongoing need for digital technology. We must not think of this as a temporary shift, but realize technology's long-term potential and value.

The Digital Evangelism and Discipleship Model in Action

The model we have outlined in this guide demonstrates how you can create relevant content that meets the spiritual and physical needs of your audience, how you can use digital technology to create communities of support, and empower churches and members to spread our messages of hope and wholeness by using digital tools. As the tools and technologies change and become more sophisticated, these principles will still apply because these are the same principles the early Church used to spread the gospel, just with modern technology. These ideas, at their core, are nothing new but are built on the shoulders of evangelist giants.

Through this guide, we have sought to expand your perceptions and show how these ideas are applicable in the modern world. It all begins with this simple model we introduced early in this guidebook.

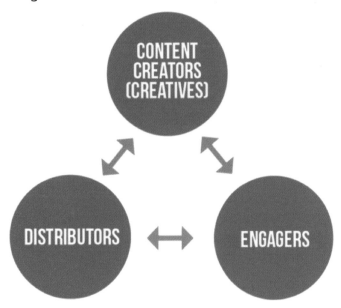

Credit: Graphic designed by Jamie Domm

If implemented at all levels of the Church, we could effectively create a thriving ecosystem online where people—at all stages in their spiritual walk—could go for growth, community, and ministry involvement, especially in times of trouble.

As we continue to adapt and modify our worship and service experiences to meet the needs and expectations of those we serve online, here is a summary of "best practices" to consider for your online church experience.

Use interactive tools. Use tools such as live chat and social media for real-time interaction. People are social creatures; let's create opportunities for social engagement online. This may feel like a distraction from the sermon, but understand that your audience (especially young people) have already been accessing social media while you preach. Digital interactive tools may be out of your comfort zone, but for many, they are a vital enhancement of their worship experience.

Rethink your service and music. Remember, put yourself in your online audience's shoes. What are they supposed to do during song service? Some may sing along, but most won't. It's awkward to watch people singing together in a building. Consider having more opportunities for special music instead and, overall, keep musical interludes brief. You can still have song service, but leave it out of the online program which also helps you avoid any **music licensing issues**[95].

Shorten the service. When restricted to online services only, don't try to fill the same amount of time as a regular church service, and limit dead space where nothing is happening. Keep the worship service moving. This principle applies to the in-person experience as well.

Speak directly to the audience. Zoom in close with the camera and let the audience see your face and your expressions. A good rule of thumb is to enable your audience to see the whites of your eyes. Speak to your audience as though you are speaking to each person individually. Acknowledge your audience, engage directly with them, and encourage comments likes, and shares. Ask them to open their Bibles and follow along with the scriptures. You can even encourage them to take notes or type in answers to your questions in the comments section of the livestream. Avoid standing alone on an empty stage with the camera zoomed out at a distance. Bringing the camera in close will make your sermon more inviting and personal.

Turn your livestream into evergreen content. When the service is over, repurpose longer videos into shorter, focused clips that will be searchable long into the future. Church announcements have a short shelf life and should not live indefinitely on your YouTube channel or website. Cut out just the message and other key elements such as the children's story to create content optimized for search. To learn how, visit the following articles on SDAdata.org:

---

95 "Copyright & Trademark Basics | Digital Evangelism | Columbia, MD." *Digital Evangelism*, www.sdadata.org/copyright-trademark-basics.html.

- **Evergreen Livestreams: 4 Ways to Turn Livestreams into Great Video Content**[96]

- **How to Start Your Own Video Ministry**[97] **(Free Course)**

Meet in the digital space. Use video conferencing technologies to keep your regular Bible studies and prayer meetings going. Zoom is a great tool. It's easy to use, and a basic account is free. You may find that your attendance increases, now that physical barriers like traffic have been removed. Refer to the guidelines provided in this book for help hosting online small groups, forums, and video conferences.

Continue to serve the community. For too long, churches have been the building up the street. During times of physical distancing, let's not allow the church to become just the empty building up the street. Church should be a group of people mobilized to serve, actively engaged in improving the well-being of their broader community, even if it is through digital interactions.

Create content to help people move along their spiritual journey. God's Church is active 24/7. Therefore, we should endeavor to put Christ on display every day through our digital influence, not just one day a week. We should create digital content that speaks to the spiritual needs of people and seeks to address their deepest longings.

Mobilize your congregation to become a reach vehicle for souls through digital door-knocking. Digital door-knocking is when a person shares spiritual content on their social media profiles or through messaging and email to create an opportunity for people to engage with them about their faith. Spiritual content can be anything (a picture, text, video, blog, etc.) and should include a personalized message. A person's friends and followers can scroll past it or choose to engage when it's convenient for them. Given that many people are stuck at home with extra time in their schedule, social media may be their main source of entertainment and connection. Create a culture of sharing and content engagement within your church community. Train your members to share your church's content (created or curated) weekly as part of ministry efforts. There's much opportunity right now for us to share and reach people everywhere using digital technologies. A congregation that understands the value of participating in ministry this way could serve as a powerful reach-vehicle for souls. Success can no longer be measured only by counting people in a building; rather, we must consider whether or not we're building a kingdom.

Create opportunities for prayer online. Even the skeptical may long for someone to care enough to pray for them personally. Social media is a powerful tool for soliciting prayer requests and following up on those requests. Prayer can be just one "like," comment, or message away. Online communication lowers the barrier to asking, making it easy for people to reach out when they may be reluctant to do so face-to-face.

---

96 "Evergreen Livestreams: 4 Ways to Turn Livestreams into Great Video Content." *Digital Evangelism*, www.sdadata.org/digital-evangelism-blog/evergreen-livestreams-4-ways-to-turn-livestreams-into-great-video-content.
97 "How to Start A Video Ministry | NAD Digital Evangelism | Columbia, MD." *Digital Evangelism*, www.sdadata.org/10commandmentsofdigitalmissions.html.

Develop a 360° community care strategy. In this time of crisis and beyond, we should work to extend the church experience beyond the confines of time and space in a building to an involved community that provides 24/7 support, not only to members but also to our broader contacts. To be effective, churches should cultivate and nurture healthy communities, both analog and digital, both within the church and in the community, thereby better positioning ourselves to provide a ministry of healing and broad networks of support.

Empower digital disciples. Content creation, engagement, and distribution are not limited to the official Church brand and accounts. Make a point of reaching out to young people, and let them know that their talents in this area are highly valued, even if they are not part of the core team. Some people just need permission and a little mentorship to realize their talents and passion for personal ministry. Everyone has social influence through texting, messenger applications, email, and social media. Encourage and inspire them to use it to build God's kingdom.

Invite creativity and new ideas. Listen to the tech savvy and to young people. Now is the time to make them feel that their spiritual gifts are valued by their church. Young people in particular are digital natives and instinctively know a great deal about how to leverage technology. They are eager to help shape the future of their church and will be more likely to stay if they are involved.

Train your members. Take the time to show your members, especially older members, how to participate and use digital tools. Ask your younger members to create tutorial videos or to FaceTime with older members to talk them through using technology for worship and ministry.

Protect your community. Going online means getting used to dealing with negative comments. For antagonists who threaten the health of your digital community, hiding/deleting comments, muting people, and even banning them are options. Refer to the section on practical tips for engagement to review the response assessment flow chart to help you navigate the sometimes rocky waters of online engagement.

Bonus: Be ready to adapt to and get comfortable with change. Change is the new normal. Embrace new ideas and technologies as they become available. Get creative, and don't be afraid to try new things. If it doesn't translate, that's okay. You will have many more chances to figure out what works. As always, pray for wisdom and guidance from the Lord as you navigate these adjustments.

We want our Church to come back stronger and more unified from the 2020 COVID-19 experience. We want our Church to emerge from this crisis ready and prepared for the future. For most of this guidebook, we've talked about how digital technologies are a powerful means to scale up traditional ministry and evangelism, but COVID-19 has pushed the need for digital technology to become our priority and possibly our long-term reality. We don't know for certain what the future will bring, but I believe that digital communications must become an integrated part of our evangelism and discipleship strategy.

The Importance of Free Speech and Why Christians Shouldn't Leave Social Media

Fulfilling Your Role in the Great Commission During Times of Censorship and Security Issues

With the recent spotlight on Mark Zuckerberg and Facebook, many users are now wondering how to respond to the revelation that the social media giant not only mishandled access to user data, but also actively suppresses expression of Christian and conservative values, playing political "favorites" throughout the world. Given that Facebook, which also owns Instagram and WhatsApp, has almost no social media competitors, it's easy to understand why most people feel upset. Facebook is the largest country in the world with **over two billion active monthly users**[98]. WhatsApp boasts over **1.5 billion monthly users**[99], and Instagram has **over 600 million monthly active users**[100]. That is an impressive share of the digital market, and the misuse of the data and/or power wielded by these platforms constitutes a formidable threat to a free society. Factor in similar revelations about Twitter, and Google (who owns YouTube), and it seems there is no "safe" platform.

However, this reach is the very reason Christians who are serious about fulfilling their role in the Great Commission should not hesitate to stay on these platforms. Social media has become part of the very fabric of our society. We can connect instantly with friends and family from around the world, share our ideas, and embrace what it means to be human. Humans, by nature, tell stories, desire connection, and share experiences and ideas. Social media platforms have saturated our lives because it speaks to these basic human needs. That need is never going away, this side of Heaven. Advancements in technology are often continually driven by this need to better communicate and connect. Think about the history of communication technology: cave drawings, smoke signals, boats, the domestication of horses, letters, the printing press, the railroad system, telegraphs, phones, cars, radio, planes, TV, the internet, social media, and whatever comes next. With each of these advancements in technology has come the advancement of the Gospel. For example, the Gutenberg printing press brought about the mass production of the Bible and religious literature, allowing the Gospel message and Reformation ideas to spread throughout Europe.

I believe the next Great Awakening will be a digital one. If we unite in purpose to spread the Gospel online, we can proclaim the Three Angels' Messages with a loud voice throughout the world. During the apostolic period, the gospel was spread by dedicated

---

98 Noyes, Dan, et al. "Top 20 Facebook Statistics - Updated May 2020." *Zephoria Inc.*, 11 May 2020, zephoria.com/top-15-valuable-facebook-statistics/.

99 Clement, J. "WhatsApp: Number of Users 2013-2017." *Statista*, 30 Apr. 2020, www.statista.com/statistics/260819/number-of-monthly-active-whatsapp-users/.

100 Carmicheal, Kayla. "Social Media Demographics for Marketers in 2020." *HubSpot Blog*, blog.hubspot.com/marketing/state-of-social-media-demographics.

teachers and evangelists who often faced ridicule, persecution and, sometimes, death. They took the gospel where the people were, regardless of the personal cost. Today, we are often hindered by fears of what people might think of us or who might be offended if we share our beliefs online for all to see. In the Western world, we do not face persecution for our religious beliefs in the same way other Christians do around the world. In the case of social media, our posts may be removed, or their reach, restricted. In some cases, expressing our religious convictions could threaten our employment. These are some less severe consequences we face as members of Western society, but it is enough to stop many of us from engaging at all. We may not be spiritually ready to stand in the fires or be persecuted like the young men in Daniel 3, but at the moment, God isn't asking us to. He has, however, asked us to use what is in our hands (Exodus 4:2) to connect with the children of God and share the gospel. With 20 million members worldwide, we, as a Church body, could work together as content creators, engagers, and distributors to generate a mighty voice for sharing the gospel message.

> *Social media is the modern School of Tyrannus, a place where the ancient Ephesians gathered to engage with new ideas, pass the time, share thought,s and participate in discussions. Paul spoke at the School of Tyrannus in Greece for two years after being kicked out of the synagogue (Acts 19:8-9), essentially getting the gospel to go viral in his day.* — Dee Casper, Director, CORE at Pennsylvania Conference of Seventh-day Adventists

"This took place for two years, so that all who lived in Asia heard the word of the Lord, both Jews and Greeks" (Acts 19:10, NASB).

People spend hours a day engaging with social media; they go there to fill time, share with friends, and see new things. Like Paul, we must take the Gospel where they are and engage them in discussion where they spend their time. We must make use of this technology before it's too late. We don't know for certain what the Time of Trouble will bring upon us, but I'm sure censorship will be a dominating factor that will lead to persecution.

I have dealt with censorship issues repeatedly while working for the North American Division. It has often shocked me and frustrated my efforts to promote life-changing medical services, healthy-living principles, spiritual messages, and services for those struggling with addiction. It has been a grave concern of mine since taking this position after my time at the Smithsonian and realizing the dramatic differences in the treatment of the content and campaigns I'm now tasked with running. This has only made me more committed than ever before to utilize these technologies to accomplish our mission. After all, if we are doing the Lord's work, the Holy Spirit will grant us favor when the algorithms won't. While our department adapts and readjusts to make social media successfully work for our mission, our goals would be better served by fair and equal treatment on the platforms.

I'm hopeful that these investigations will ultimately result in making Facebook, as well as other giants like YouTube and Twitter, a safe place for free speech, religious expression, and the exchange of all ideas. Religious organizations will stand to benefit from the removal of discriminatory biases that limit the reach of, and access to, the advertisements of our ideas and resources.

The outcome of these legal inquiries will undoubtedly shape the future. These investigations are ultimately about every individual's Constitutional right to free speech, religious expression, and privacy of personal information. Please invest the time to understand the implications of these platforms' breaches of trust. We must pay attention and hold these companies accountable; otherwise, they maintain monopolies with the power to decide who has a voice, who has your data, and what they do with this information. Not only is this problematic in a free society, but also problematic to our mission as Seventh-day Adventists.

As Christians, we must continue to advocate for free speech. Our ability to spread the gospel in a public forum relies upon it. As efforts to censor Christian viewpoints online and in the public space intensify, we may be tempted to respond defensively in a way that doesn't represent the character of Christ. However, Jesus calls us to be a practical witness, one that puts Him on display in all aspects of our lives, one that is not so easily censored. Jesus sought first to fulfill people's needs; He then invited them to follow. We can use our digital and social influence to gain insights and focus on meeting the mental, physical, and spiritual needs of those around us. Once relationships and trust are built, we can invite them to "taste and see that the Lord is good" (Psalm 34:8, NIV). The gospel of action can further our ministry of hope and wholeness, even when words of truth are silenced. Regardless of what (if anything) ultimately comes out of these inquiries, we must press forward and speak Bible truths with this powerful technology. Stay, but stay with purpose. Share your faith online as long as you can.

Our integrity, genuine care for others, honor, and faith in Christ can never be taken from us. Our prayers cannot be blocked from reaching God. Christ's character can never be shut down. By embracing the attitude of a servant first and apologist second, light will shine through us to draw others to the God we represent.

Where Is Your God Now? God on the Move in Times of Crisis

The weekend that the world woke up to the COVID-19 pandemic saw a wave of closings and radical changes to our daily lives never seen in the history of mankind. The same weekend brought a stunning amount of anti-Christian rhetoric online. I am an administrator for over 50 ministry social media accounts, and my notifications were filled with hateful comments, aggressively mocking us and our collective faith and, in some cases, even blaming Christians and our "foolish" thinking through some convoluted logic that I didn't bother to try to understand. What shook me most was that this behavior was foretold in the Bible. It wasn't that I didn't believe the Scriptures, but in my mind, it was always for some far, future time. I certainly wasn't expecting to experience this first-hand on March 15, 2020.

> *Know this first of all, that in the last days, mockers will come with their mocking, following after their own lusts, and saying, "Where is the promise of His coming? For ever since the fathers fell asleep, all continues just as it was from the beginning of creation" (2 Peter 3:3-4).*

One repeated phrase stuck out for me as I combed through the comments, deleting them and banning hostile people to protect our faith communities from continued harassment in this time of crisis. I lost count of how many times I read, "Where is your God now?" Repeatedly, I saw the same comment, sometimes accompanied by rude pictures mocking our Savior. The hostility from these armchair antagonists was deeply concerning.

But the question remains, "Where is my God now?" In the days that followed, I began to see an immense amount of creativity and innovation emerging from the Church as pastors and ministry leaders began to adapt.

> *I realized that the answer to the mockers' question is that my God is on the move, while we're stuck at home.*

When fleeing persecution, the early Church took the gospel to new regions out of necessity. Two thousand years later, we find ourselves in a similar situation. Out of necessity, we must now take the gospel message to the digital mission field and spread our message of hope and wholeness when it is needed most.

"We know that God causes all things to work together for good to those who love God, to those who are called according to His purpose" (Romans 8:28, NAS 1977).

In Daniel 3, God didn't deliver the three Hebrew boys from the fire; He delivered them IN the fire to act as witnesses to King Nebuchadnezzar and his kingdom. While in the fire, the three boys came near to God and walked with the preincarnate Christ. Their experience served a greater purpose and testifies to us even today. God didn't create the fire, the persecution or the pestilence, but He can steer His Church in this crisis to accomplish His will for the salvation of souls. He can and will manifest His power so that the living may know that the Most High rules over mankind (see Daniel 4:17).

When it appears that the world is falling apart and people are paralyzed with fear, where is God? God is on the move in every church and in the heart of every missionary stepping out in faith to accomplish our mission by any means necessary. He doesn't need us to fulfill His work, but He invites us to work alongside the Holy Spirit. For digital advocates like me, this is a long-awaited, surprising answer to prayer.

It's unfortunate that it took a pandemic to motivate the Church to embrace digital technologies on a large scale. For people who know that the end is coming, we have dragged our feet too long. COVID-19 is a kick in our complacency and a wake-up call to jump on the digital bandwagon. We have had access to these tools for over a decade, and I believe the Holy Spirit has been pleading with us to use them. Previously, many of us advocated for rethinking church in the digital age to meet the needs and expectations of younger generations. Our voices were often dismissed as too extreme. Overnight, the landscape changed; now, we are forced to rethink church without the building for everyone. Perhaps this is the point. We've gotten too accustomed to thinking of church as a place to go to for a few hours a week, not as people in action, striving to improve the well-being of others and spreading the Good News.

Now is the time to focus on the future and on what the Church can become. Until now, those of us advocating for digital technologies have been up against systems and traditions that have been difficult to change. However, these structures and mindsets are quickly becoming obsolete in this new reality. The current generation no longer has the option of embracing change or leaving it to the next generation. The time is now; otherwise, we will become irrelevant. Change is never easy, but anything is possible with the Lord (see Matthew 19:26).

This shock to our society is nothing to fear. God is always with us, and we must continue to embrace this new reality to continue the work. Make no mistake, we are never going back—COVID-19 will fundamentally change how businesses, organizations, and society functions. Everyone across the generations will be forced to utilize digital tools for productivity and daily life. When the crisis is over and we can once again embrace our brothers and sisters, we will all have to tighten our belts from the economic fallout. Travel will be a luxury, while the positive impact on the environment may solidify many of our behavioral changes.

Only God knows for sure how this will change the world, but the Bible tells us that this is only the beginning of the birth pains. There is more pestilence and tribulation to come. We may never fully be able to leave physical distancing behind, but time spent in physical isolation can be filled with seeking for truth and assurance in our messages of hope and wholeness. People will continue to turn to the internet for companionship, understanding, information, anonymity, and more. We must be the voice that answers back, online, in these times of crisis and beyond.

COVID-19 is not the end, but it is a warning—a warning to God's Church to wake up and get ready. Jesus is coming, and we haven't finished the work. This crisis is an opportunity to prepare and mobilize. It's time for a generation of digital evangelists and disciples to carry the gospel to the digital mission field, which may well be the final mission field. This is our generation's Great Commission.